A GOOD ENOUGH DAD

A GOOD ENOUGH DAD

The True Confessions
of an Infant Father

NIGEL PLANER

Illustrations by Nigel Planer

BCA

LONDON · NEW YORK · SYDNEY · TORONTO

This edition published 1992 by BCA
by arrangement with Ebury Press
an imprint of the Random Century Group
Random Century House
20 Vauxhall Bridge Road
London SW1V 2SA

CN 6011

Designed by: Bob Vickers
Illustrated by: Nigel Planer

Typeset in Trump Mediaeval by Textype, Cambridge
Printed and bound in Great Britain by
Mackays of Chatham Plc, Kent

DEDICATION

The fact that I got to be the one who writes about parent-hood in a book when she actually had the baby, pissed off Anna, Stanley's mum, somewhat, and I can see why. Not only would I not be a dad, and Stanley not be a Stanley, without her, but also this book would not have been possible without her advice, help and sometimes downright indignation.

INTRODUCTION

I read in a movie mag that Arnold Schwarzenegger, while developing a film in which he plays *the first man ever to give birth*, was preparing for his role by walking around in an 'Empathy Belly', a new strap-on product from America for New Age fathers to get an understanding of what being pregnant is like. It's a pregnancy-simulating harness for men which creates what the maker calls 'gut-level' awareness by putting pressure on the abdomen and bladder, and by creating foetal kicking movements. Comes with matching maternity smock, of course. In fact, Arnie will not be the first prosthetic father: Marcello Mastroianni made a film in the sixties where he gave birth, and, in 1990, I was in *Frankenstein's Baby*, a BBC film in which I gave birth. This makes Arnie the *third man ever to give birth*, but that won't sound so good on his press release.

It is scientifically just about possible for a man to bear a child these days, assisted by about as much technology as an Apollo moon landing, but on the whole, men have to cope with parenthood of a much more mundane, and non-prosthetic, kind. You know, where the women actually have the babies, and the men get to spout off in the pub about how much it's changed their lives.

I suppose I should have called this book *Baby Bore*, then I could have sold the film rights to Sylvester Stallone or Jack Nicholson. Just picture it now: 'Bruce Willis in *Baby Bore Two*', in which a hugely tough gunslinging famous person gets left alone with a baby for half an hour, and discovers, through having to change his first nappy, how to be a more fulfilled human being, how to create world peace, and how to keep his picture in *Hello!* magazine on a regular basis.

I envy Warren Beatty, who said in a recent interview about expecting his first child: 'I don't have any negative feelings about it, only elation.' Obviously, he generously left all the natural negative feelings about it for his partner, Annette Bening, to handle. There seems to be a plethora of fifty-year-old first-time fathers in Hollywood at the moment. Have they all been waiting to have children until becoming a dad was fashionable enough? Reading the tabloids, it would be forgivable to imagine that it was Warren, not Annette, who was going to have eight pounds of human flesh and bone pass through him.

Women already have role models, not just good-mother, earth-mother, long-suffering-mother role models, but now hard-hitting-professional role models, top-executive role models, I'm-free-to-drive-my-Vauxhall-Astra-wherever-I-want role models. So far, men don't have much in the way of fatherly role models. I suppose there are Bill Cosby and Alf Garnet, but apart from that, take your pick from Woody Allen, John Major, Mick Jagger, Paul Daniels or Simon le Bon. Personally, I don't like the idea of Schwarzenegger being an example of good fatherhood any more than I like the soppy, dungaree-clad home-husband social-worker image. The point is that men can't really share childbirth with women, and the nappy-changing, food-splattering, getting-up-at-night stage, if you think about it, only goes on for a fortieth of your child's life. It's the remaining sixty-odd years, when the child is still your child and you're going to have to adjust to it, that scares the pants off many first-time fathers.

I have reached the conclusion that there is a deliberate conspiracy of silence to keep men in the dark about fatherhood, because if/they actually knew, in their randy twenties, what they were letting themselves in for, they might be put off sex, have vasectomies at their bar mitzvahs, or superglue condoms on to their willies.

NO APOLOGIES

In almost every baby and child-raising book I can find, the baby is always assumed to be a boy and referred to as 'he'. In the more modern baby books they usually print a little apology for doing this before the introduction. They're only calling the baby 'he' to differentiate it from the mother, or because 'it' sounds so terrible. They bemoan the fact that there isn't a better pronoun than 'it' to imply a person without specifying gender. In *Babywatching*, Desmond Morris uses 'it', but feels he has to apologise: 'No insult to babies intended'. John Cleese and Robin Skynner in their book *Families and How to Survive Them*, say they refer to all babies and children as 'he', but 'not for any sexist reason'. In *The Good Enough Parent*, Bruno Bettelheim goes one better and refers to both the child and the mother as 'he', claiming he is using the masculine pronoun as a generic term because he is too traditional to go 'he/she-ing' and 'talking about persons'. It does, however, seem a bit tough on the mother to be referred to as 'he', especially as Bettelheim continues: 'While both parents contribute significantly to a child's being raised well (or not so well), it is the mother, particularly during the early years, who is apt to play a considerably more important role in the process'. Miriam Stoppard, ever the champion of working mothers and quality time, was the only one I found who, in her *Pregnancy and Birth Handbook*, referred to the baby as 'she' throughout, and although I confess I found it strange at first, I got used to it after a page or two, and did not become confused about whether she was referring to the mother, the child, the midwife, the obstetrician, or the cleaning person.

I'm dwelling on this because it's in the business of having children that gender, and expected sexual roles, take on frightening significance. From the sex of the expected child to who will do what over the next twenty years until it becomes an adult. It's through and for rearing children that we define ourselves as male or female. It may be screamingly obvious, but there are so few pregnancy books for men, because men don't get pregnant. In fact, the only one I could find was *Fathering for Men* by Martin Francis, whose advice was sensible despite its stupid title. So, in this book, I make no apologies for referring throughout to my son as 'he', myself as 'I', my wife, my mother, and various aunts and ex-girlfriends as 'she', and all other men on earth as 'them'.

GOOD ENOUGH

This book has been written over the course of eighteen months, and although, during that time, I have stayed roughly the same person, Stanley, of course, has not. Time certainly doesn't fly when you're two. Everything is significant and new. As I've watched him growing, I've changed my mind many times about what it is I'm witnessing, and about what it is I should be doing – what constitutes being 'A Good Enough Dad'.

During Anna's pregnancy, although I was concerned about her and the child's physical well-being, and tried my hardest to get as involved as her in Fallopian tubes, Micturition, Amenorrhoea and Quickening, I must admit that what kept me awake at night was not worrying about breast feeding or breech births, but accommodation, money, family relationships, and the future. And for Stanley's sake, I'm glad that it did. If I was a little embryo waiting to be born, it would feel good to know that not only did I have someone concerned with whether I was breathing or not, but also someone else concerned about my place in the world later on.

The concept of the 'Good Enough Parent' was espoused by the child psychologists D. W. Winnicott and

Bruno Bettelheim, but it's not some heavy, meaningful philosophy. It's quite simple, and rather obvious when you think about it. In struggling to be a good mother or father, you may try to make up for inadequacies you think you see in your own parents and upbringing, so that your child may never have the sort of difficulties you yourself had. Circumstances vary. It might mean being more constant with your own children, more physically demonstrative, less demonstrative, richer. If you take a child's-eye view for a moment, however, it is not confidence-inducing, for instance, to be enveloped with conscious, premeditated physical love, or conscious, premeditated anything. It is an uncomfortable responsibility to know that a parent is giving up too much for you. A child does not want 'too good' parents any more than it wants negligent or absent parents. It wants parents who pay enough attention, and then stop and go and do something to please themselves. The greatest skills for the 'Good Enough' parent to acquire, as any working mother will tell you, are all rather undramatic sounding: 'Sticking around', 'Being quite patient', 'Leaving alone', 'Muddling through'.

ROLLER COASTER

There is a brilliant scene at the end of Ron Howard's *Parenthood*, when Steve Martin, playing a harassed and frazzled Dad, goes to see his son in the school play. He wants his boy to excel, but the play starts to go wrong. Suddenly, with full Hollywood special effects, we see, from the point of view of Steve Martin's character, that the whole thing is starting to sway and swirl, and we are on a fast and furious roller coaster. The father character is apprehensive at first. We suspect he may be having a nervous breakdown. But then, holding hands with his wife, he gradually learns to enjoy the dizzy-making movement and sway with it. Like a passenger leaning into a turn on

11

a motor cycle, the more you try and resist or control it, the more likely you are to cause a crash. This final scene in *Parenthood* just about sums it up as far as I'm concerned. I wish I'd thought of it.

ONE

Letter to My Son to be Opened When He Becomes a Father, and Not Before.

January, 1991

Dear Stan,

Sorry about the secrecy in these matters so far, but I thought it better that there were certain things you didn't know until you were definitely going to become a dad yourself. You have to be mad to have children. The less you know about what it will really be like, the better, otherwise no one would ever do it. I was certainly in total, and blissful, ignorance until you arrived on 5 September 1988. So that's why this time-capsule, sealed envelope containing all the letters I wrote you from blob to toddler, is only to be opened on the day a woman looks at you and says, 'I've got something to tell you, and I don't mean I forgot to take the videos back again.' Up until then, I will subscribe to the healthy romantic lie, the conspiracy of silence that has kept the human race going so far.

Try to imagine your pa as a young man (well, quite young) all the way back in 1988, when fatherhood was considered so trendy that they actually asked him to write a book about it. Male Hollywood stars couldn't be seen in the glossy pages of gossip magazines without sporting a baby of some sort; articles on the women's pages of daily newspapers were mostly about men, and mostly read by them; every sitcom on telly had to have a reformed medallion man aching to care for a child; and the movie business became 'Daddy obsessed'.

Yes, around the time you were born, believe it or not, having children had become, momentarily, a fashion

13

must. *And being a daddy was suddenly the subject of a neurotic journalistic feeding frenzy. Have we been getting it right for five thousand years? ran the thinking. Well obviously not. There are still wars, there's still pollution, there's still crime and violence, and game shows on TV. Maybe it's bad fathering that's been to blame all along. Maybe that's why the human race is so messed up, maybe that explains male aggression, rape, the ozone hole, and Jeremy Beadle. It's a lack of proper fathering, that's what it is. The issue suddenly became urgent, and a lot of money was spent on it.*

Imagine your New Age, caring, sharing dad at home. He is wearing a comfy, but expensive, chunky woollen cardigan. His hair is soft but well kept, and he doesn't have any double chins or dry skin patches. He has a body that is the result of several months' combined gym and sun-lamp work, and he's living in a nice spacious semidetached house, with nice furniture, and nice decorations. There's even some nice chaotic mess around. Not the kind of sticky, grimy, irremovable mess that you and I know so well, but New Age mess, a few cushions out of place, a few toys on the floor. The sort of mess about which you'd say 'God, sorry about the mess' to all your house guests, and they'd all reply 'Don't worry, you should see our place'. Beverley Craven is playing somewhere in the background, or Dire Straits, or even Carly Simon, and 'thirtysomething' is flickering

on the TV screen. *Outside on the drive is this man's
astonishingly clean Renault or BMW or Rover or
Vauxhall, a sexy-but-not-too-macho car, with a neat
baby seat in the front/back, and, amazingly, absolutely
no takeaway food cartons on the passenger seat, no
over-full ashtrays, no broken toys, sweets, sweet papers,
or old clothes.*

Doesn't really sound like your dad one bit, does it?

*Your mum, by the way, is away, of course, otherwise
why all that jolly but not obnoxious mess in our living
room as I try to feed, entertain and change possibly the
cutest, and cheekiest, baby in the entire world, or at
least out of the two hundred or so babies who
auditioned for the part (you). As the food spluts merrily
on to my soft woollen cardigan, I become exasperated,
in a sort of 'End of Part One' hwa hwa hwaaaa way, like
I don't really mind, I just hope I can keep my house in
order until my wife returns from the power-dressed
executive computer commercial on the other channel
and gives that exasperated sort of 'End of Part One' hwa
hwa hwaaaa look that wives always do in commercials
to say they don't really mind either. Maybe she's having
an affair with the man from the coffee ad, I don't know,
I must ask her one day. Possibly a good moment to
mention it would be the next time we playfully splosh
paste and paint over each other as we do all our own
wallpaper hanging and decorating together (rag-rolled of*

course). I correct my wife, but not aggressively, when people ask her about which month baby did what, because, of course, I can remember all those little things better than she can. I wake up in the night, I change the nappies, I cook, wash up, hoover, decorate (with partner), drive, feed baby and, above all, care. And all of this without losing the essential masculinity that my expensive shower-shampoo-conditioner-and-aftershave set bestows on me. I'm such a good father, I could go on chat shows about it, and say interesting and original things like, 'Oh, it's changed my life'. Of course, my children smell sweet all the time, and my back never aches from lifting them up...

Aaargh. Aaarrrgh! AAARRRGHHH!!!

HOW DID I GET HERE?

It's late at night. I'm sitting in the shower room with my notebook on my lap. A half-drunk can of Guinness is balancing on the soap dish where I can reach it easily, and I use the now defunct plughole as an ashtray. Since the birth of Stanley, the shower room has trebled as office, smoking room and den (he has hijacked the second bedroom, of course). I must be careful not to make too much noise, lest I wake the baby, or the mother for that matter, so I'd better not write anything funny, in case I get the giggles.

I remember this shower room when it could have been described as 'ensuite'. Before we ripped out the basin and shower fittings to make room for my books, my guitar, and the old dentist's filing cabinet that now contains every folder and piece of paper pertaining to my former life. Thirty years of scribblings, and me, crammed into eight foot by three. In a minute, I'll creep back into the bedroom in the dark, and try to find the bed without banging my shins on the furniture, and get into it as quickly as possible so as not to deprive her of even seconds of what has become the most precious commodity in our lives: sleep. I remember when I could have taken a shower here around this time, and then padded into what is now the nursery dressed only in a towel, smoking a cigarette, drunk, even, if I had wanted to be, strummed a few idle chords or put on a cassette, and then sat down at the word processor (yes, I had room for one then) to write this.

Oh yes, I remember those bachelor days. Waking whenever, and then lying in bed for an hour or more just thinking about when to get up. Whether to get up. If I was hungry, I could have strolled into the kitchen, where there would have been piles of dirty dishes and it wouldn't have mattered, and I could have cut myself a slice of bread and casually left the bread knife out, on the floor, even. And the electric points could have been left switched on and gaping open and it wouldn't have been the end of the world, except environmentally speaking, of course. And being up this late would have been silly, possibly, because of work in the morning, but it wouldn't have been the complete kamikaze decision it is tonight, when I know that there are those three hours before work tomorrow when I'll have to try to stop too much of the 'num nums' from landing on the floor, and convince Stanley by stealth and inventiveness that taking all of the saucepans out of the cupboard and playing drums with them is not a reasonable thing to do at a quarter to seven in the morning; when I'll have to use every bit of comic timing I have to keep him still long enough to get him nappied up without dropping little bits of poo on the carpet.

Oh yes, those were the days. Days when I thought life insurance was something comedians advertised on television, not paid a monthly banker's order to. Days when I thought baby-sitters only appeared in sitcoms, when I could stay late at work because I felt like it, when I though appointment diaries were mere fashion accessories. Days when I could leave a Biro in every room in case an idea needed jotting down on paper rather than on the walls. Days when I thought school was something you are meant to revisit ten years later and sneer at, not something you are meant to look around two years before.

I'd never even picked up a baby until four years ago. My first tentative step in that direction was with my nephew, who was lying on the floor screaming his head off. I had read somewhere that they like being walked; in other words, being carried around by someone who is walking at a steady pace. Evidently, the gentle side-to-side motion puts them in touch genetically with their nomadic forebears, well, that's what this article had said. More importantly, it stops them crying. It also reminds

18

them of the time not so long ago when they were rolling around in the dark in thick juices swaying from side to side like a bubble in a spirit level. Hence rocking cradles, hence ballroom dancing, hence rock and roll.

I decided to try it and it worked. I walked up and down the kitchen for half an hour with him and he was quiet. I put him down and he started screaming again. After this experiment, I thought I'd pretty well got child-rearing, and baby care, licked. As long as I had legs, and there was space to walk, no problems. I considered myself fully equipped and trained in the unlikely event of these skills ever being required again. And up until that year I had thought it unlikely that they ever would be. I had never seen myself as a father-type person. I had been involved only in the Mars Bar philosophy of life: Work, Rest and Play. (My Work, My Rest, My Play.) *Not* having children had been the cement of any long-standing relationships so far. If people asked me didn't I want to have children? I had stock replies, such as 'Not when you see what they turn into', or 'Not until the world is a safer place', or 'Not until I'm rich'. No, I had certainly been in no hurry to multiply; propagation was very low on my list of priorities. But then taking your time over this is truly an unfair advantage that men have over women. Charlie Chaplin sired a child when he was seventy-seven, so they say. (A bit unfortunate for the child when it was three and needed throwing in the air and catching, but possible nonetheless.)

Biology is cruel on women, however, and many career women go past their sell-by-date before they have started a family. Have them too old, and it is physically riskier for the child and for yourself; too young, and you may find yourself frustrated with so much responsibility early on. Statistically, a woman is at her biological high point, child bearing-wise, at the age of twenty-two. Not necessarily the best time if she also wants to have some life of her own. It is an impossible thing to get right, or to plan. For women, having children is rather like the British film industry; by the time the script is right, the money has dropped out; when the new money is found, the star is unavailable; by the time the whole deal is in place, your option on the novel has run out anyway, or someone else has done something along similar lines.

It has its advantages, though, I am told. You get to create life, for a start. This may account for a certain amount of smugness in some women, and explain why they have this uncanny quality, often mystified, idolised, or defiled by men, of actually knowing what life is really about.

So, four years ago I had never picked up a baby. Not only that, but I'd never really noticed them either. They must have been there I suppose, but they'd never registered. Like an item which is lost and then suddenly turns up right in front of your eyes on the table where you first looked. When friends of mine had them, I made all the right noises, I even visited hospitals with flowers and congratulations cards, and looked into those transparent plastic boxes where newborns are generally kept with a warm smile on my face certainly, and with appropriate cooing goo-goo noises, but it was the kind of interest that, to be honest, wore off within a minute or so of leaving the hospital ward.

All that was before, by chance, my one-year-old niece came to live in our flat with her mum and dad for a few weeks, and my sitting room was suddenly full of rusks and rattles, clothes drying on the radiator, piles of plastic equipment, and the kitchen was invaded by strange-shaped sterilised bottles. My little niece was the first baby I had ever really noticed. I noticed her because she made sure I did. In whatever room I was at peace, she would seek me out on a high-speed crawling mission. She was the first baby I met who had a sense of humour, or, at any rate, the first baby whose humour I was forced to appreciate. Like most of us, she thought being naughty was funny. She thought hiding in my dustbin was funny. She thought scribbling on my scripts and pushing random buttons on my computer was funny. And I suppose it must have been. Having my concentration and relaxation so easily disarmed by these search and destroy missions of hers was my first proper introduction to the world of the under-fives. She was relentless in her persistence, and taught me that as far as a baby is concerned, if a joke is good, it's worth repeating, and repeating, and repeating.

So, having been forced to notice one child, I began to notice all the others. In the street, in the supermarket, in passing cars. Suddenly, there were babies everywhere – well, they'd been there all along obviously, but I was amazed. I noticed that friends of mine had parties in the daytime, to which I was not often invited, where children would meet and jump up and down on inflatable castles. I noticed that bosses, agents, doctors and anyone sitting behind a desk usually had a photo of some of these miniature people on top of it. I noticed how, when I was on tour doing a spoof rock and roll act, the wives, girlfriends, tour managers, coach drivers, caterers and even roadies preferred to stay on the tour bus watching the drummer's son having his nappy changed than stand in the wings watching our band show off on stage. I wouldn't say I was getting broody. I just noticed that's all.

I noticed that both my brothers and most of my friends were now parents. That some of my hair had turned grey. That if I went out in the evening I was often the oldest person there, but when among people of my own age I would behave like the youngest. I wouldn't say broody, but I did start making plans for extensively redecorating the flat.

There was, of course, another event at around this time that did far more to tip the balance of my mind into the insanity of parenting. I met Anna and turned overnight (no, quicker than that) from a cautious, thoughtful kind of person into a netless trapeze artist, a Red Devil without a parachute, a member of the Dangerous Sports Club. I sometimes think that we have no choice in this. What we suppose to be our own feelings really belong to the two halves of a new person demanding to come together. Our choices are limited by the conscious decisions of the unborn generation. As if the spirit of young Stanley was hovering in the ether, saying, 'I think I'll have that one, and, er . . . that one.'

All the way home in the car, I am thinking of that little white Biro-sized stick of plastic. Will it have changed colour? I know from the look on her face when I get in that it has. She shows it to me without saying anything. The tip of it has gone a sort of pale smoky blue. We look at each other in silence. I am thinking, 'Does this mean it's going to be a boy? Does it turn pink if it's a girl?' But I don't say anything. For once, I realise this is not the time for silly jokes. We sit down. I come up with what is, for me, an amazingly sensible suggestion. That neither of us should be the first to say what our reaction to the news is. Instead, we should, on a count of three, simultaneously say what we think. This way we can avoid influencing each other's true feelings. I don't want the baby to be a product of misunderstandings and obligations from the word go. She says, 'I know what I think already,' I say, 'Don't tell me . . . One, two, three, brilliant!'

The man in the off-licence who sold me the champagne three minutes later must have wondered why I had such a stupid grin on my face. Back upstairs in the flat, as I pour us both a second glass of celebratory alcohol, she has to cope with the conflicting demands which will be with her for the rest of her life. Let's get pissed and celebrate, versus, I shouldn't drink too much for the baby. She abstained, so I ended up drinking most of the champagne and getting more drunk than I intended. So begins the polarisation of the roles we will have to play.

MARSHMALLOWLAND

The other day I heard a builder on a site whistling the first few bars of the theme tune to *Postman Pat*. When he got to the 'and his black-and-white cat' bit, he recognised the tune he was so publicly and absent-mindedly broadcasting, became self-conscious and quickly changed it into a free-form improvisation around a Rolling Stones-type riff. We've all had to do this. This is what people mean when they say that if you spend too much time with your kids, your mind will turn to jelly.

But the jellification starts much earlier than Postman Pat delivering his letters 'just as day is dawning'. It starts roughly in the second week of your partner's pregnancy, and continues to accelerate until the third or fourth birthday of your child, by which time you are living in Marshmallowland. Beyond that I have no experience, so I am unable to report back about whether life is sustainable in Marshmallowland, and whether the marshmallowy thoughts you have there lead to any kind of constructive behaviour other than 'Let's have another one'.

We decide not to tell anyone for the first two months, as this is the most likely time for something to go wrong. The next day we each tell everybody we meet, and when we see each other in the evening, both say 'I thought we agreed not to tell anybody.'

People's reactions vary tremendously. On the whole, the men's reactions to my news can be divided into two: the ones who don't yet have children: 'Oh dear oh dear oh dear, rather you than me mate, it's the beginning of the end, there's your manhood gone down the drain', (in other words, basic envy), and the ones who do have children: 'How absolutely incredible, what fantastic news, how is your wife/partner taking it? Oh it'll definitely change your life for the better' (in other words, I'm so glad you decided to join me in this bottomless hole.

Here, have a syringeful of my heroin). The women's reactions to Anna telling them tend to be more complicated. They range from: 'Your tits will sag, he'll never look at you sexually ever again, I don't think you're ready, what about your career?' (basic envy again), through: 'How marvellous, sit down, I'll look after you, I'm going to be by your side right through this' (genuine friendship, admiration and love, with a teeny little streak of envy), to complete silence and never getting in touch ever again (major panic).

Every day a new pregnancy book seems to materialise in the flat. When you pick up a newspaper, there's a pregnancy book under it. When you get into bed, your feet bang against a childbirth encyclopaedia. Every conversation seems to be about how she's feeling. Has she been sick today? How is her saliva tasting? I don't know how some women manage to work right up to the last minute, because the baby in there swallows her energy by the shovelful. She is tired all the time. I, on the other hand, am fretful and panicky. Over the next few months I watch her body transform itself slowly into a baby-making machine, like a rather bad special effect in a low-budget horror movie. I take a Polaroid picture every five weeks or so to remind us. She looks more and more beautiful, but is convinced she looks less and less so. It's a relief for her when it sticks out far enough to be obviously pregnant, rather than possibly just fat.

We visit baby shops and buy neutral-coloured vests and tiny all-in-ones for the baby. A male customer in the baby shop, with two children of his own, cracks bar room jokes at me about how the baby will ruin me financially. Anna is upset by this. She seems to cry nowadays at the flip of a coin. I am upset, too, but if I am jumpy in these first few months, she is a waterfall of emotions, with a fast-forward and rewind facility. She has an excuse, of course. Her hormones are going through glasnost, coup, revolution and independence all at once. Mine aren't.

PREGNANCY: ABOUT THE MOTHER

Unlike the rest of literature, where women constantly have to play the role of ciphers to men, and are judged by how men see them, when it comes to pregnancy and pregnancy books, the roles are reversed. We get half a chapter, or a paragraph, usually about how understanding we're going to have to be, and how instead of bringing home bottles from the off-licence, we should be bringing home bottles of 'essential oils', and learning to give soothing gentle all-over massages without getting too turned on by it. Since this is a baby book for men, I think it's only fair that I should give half a chapter or so to the woman and what she is going through while the man is carrying on the really important work of reverting to infantile behaviour, whining, whingeing, going out for special food requests, and bragging about it in the pub.

Just about every bit of a woman's body, and body chemistry, undergoes a change during pregnancy and birth. Some of these changes are permanent, some are not. When you go into it, women must be bonkers to want to do it, and one can appreciate why they get so pissed off with men for not having to go through this. Men, on the other hand, are all just spare pricks, really, constantly haunted by the fact that they're just not as valuable to the human race as women are. During pregnancy a women can suffer from any or all of the following: backache, piles, varicose veins, skin pigmentation changes, bleeding gums, severe heartburn, vomiting, nosebleeds, nasal congestion, headaches, muscle cramps, abdominal pain, unbelievable tiredness, indigestion, horrid-tasting saliva, swelling of the face, fingers and feet, carpal tunnel syndrome in the wrist (painful), cystitis, insomnia and stretch marks – oh, and also their bones go all soft. Among some of the changes she undergoes which may be permanent are those to the teeth, hair, posture, bladder, cervix, uterus, bowels and skin. The list seems endless. And this is before we've even started on the emotional and personality changes. We men may think it's a very modern thing to say that having a child has 'changed our lives', but for a woman this is not a matter of choice or fashion. Just the idea of something growing inside you is enough to create, in some women, a degree of emotional instability, anxiety, irritability and depression. I know it would me.

Then there's the worry that she might not be any good at it: the baby might die, or she might die; the baby might not be a very nice person, and nor might she by the time she's gone through all this. Plus, 90 per cent of old wives, helpful aunts, friends and doctors agree that actually getting the baby out of her in nine months' time is going to hurt rather a lot. To cap it all, she's got a partner who's freaking out about no longer being very important, or, worse, traipsing around after her with bottles of essential oils, trying to be understanding, or going off to work, completely ignoring her and eyeing up other women. It must be impossible to believe, as she swells up to a ridiculous size, that actually, by some magic, to her partner, she looks even sexier like this than before.

She's not meant to drink, smoke, take drugs or violent exercise. She's meant to clump about and bloom. She has to go and see doctors and experts who measure her weight gain. She has to listen to endless advice from other women who've had babies, to horror stories of labours that went on for over a week. She may suffer from constipation, flatulence and vaginal discharge, but she is no longer allowed the curries and lager that made these worthwhile

It is an absolute miracle that so many women manage to get through this at all – some also holding down jobs until the last minute – let alone do it several times over and actually enjoy it. I couldn't even get through reading the books about it. I gave up when I got to the chapters on 'chronic polyhydramnios' and 'pre-eclampsia', whatever they are. There's the concern about the 'lie' of the baby: the 'longitudinal lie' (sideways), the 'oblique lie' (something Shakespearian no doubt), and the 'extended cephalic version'. There's so much to worry about. The 'presentation' of the baby: has the head engaged or will it be a 'breech' presentation (feet first), with the baby coming out screaming 'A horse, a horse, my kingdom for a horse'? Luckily for Anna and me, the only 'abnormalities in the passage' we experienced during Stanley's birth were me having a quick cigarette in the hospital corridor.

While she is pregnant, she will have to put up not only with completely unsympathetic people who barge in front of her in queues when her feet feel like masked potatoes, total bastards who drive straight over zebra crossings when she has only just lowered herself gingerly off the kerb, and assorted pushers, shovers and glarers, but also with patronising do-gooders who tell her, 'You shouldn't be carrying those heavy bags in your condition', show-offs who try to help her cross the road as if she were a five-year-old, and men who make short speeches about how difficult and worthy a task motherhood is, and then instantly turn their backs on her and continue to talk to everyone but her about work, or sport, or anything but motherhood. Yes, she will have to learn to cope with both kinds of taxi driver: the one who tells her to 'Fuck off' when she is standing in the rain with heavy shopping, and the one who treats her with excessive and overdone care, enveloping her in cotton wool like a precious jewel, as if being pregnant was the one and only time a woman merits any respect, or even attention.

From the moment her bump starts to show, she will learn what it is like to have people look straight through her, seeing her no longer as a person but as something carrying a person. She has had her first taste of what it's like to be less important than someone else. Men take much longer to have this sensation. Sometimes they never get there and spend their entire lives running away from it, determined to live forever on planet Me. But then they don't have the crash course in Unselfishness Studies that women's bodies put them through, so it's understandable.

After she's had it, apart from being encumbered with a ludicrous amount of paraphernalia, weird-shaped bottles, nappies, changing-tables, mobiles and carrycots, her body continues to be used like a service and is the subject of discussion and scrutiny for months to come. Her breasts become part of a political wrangle: 'Breast or bottle'? And if breast, should she feed openly in public? There are organisations to defend her right to whip out a tit on public transport if she so wishes ('Breastfeeding Without Stigma', 'Hidden Assets', 'La Lèche League'). There are shopkeepers and restaurant owners who will throw her out if she does.

The most frustrating thing is that despite all of this, more often than not she will be overcome by joy and feelings of satisfaction, fulfilment and wonder. So despite the appalling deal she's getting, she feels good about herself. Imagine what damage this paradox must do to what she had hitherto thought of as her self-esteem!

Over the next few months, events which might seem major to her, like baby's first smile, or tooth, do not make headline news, not even a mention in the small ads, and she may start to feel cut off from the world. Just her and baby. And to begin with it's good that she does because the baby really does need her full-time attention. But then some reconstructed New Age new man steps in and starts bonding all over the place, putting the nappy-rash cream back in a different drawer and thinking he's great just because he's managed to burp the baby. And everyone else seems to think he's great too, and every time she opens a woman's magazine there are more pictures of smug showbiz gits in linen suits holding their babies, while the mothers stand by blinking at the camera like disturbed nocturnal animals. Oh yes, we've come a long way, haven't we, since Marie Stopes, the mother of modern birth control, wrote in 1918: 'Every woman who has picked her mate freely, and because she thought him a knight among men, must long to see his characteristics reproduced so that the world should not lose the imprint of his splendour.'

he's fallen asleep on me, what do I do now?

TWO

Dear Embryo

At the moment I don't know whether you're going to be a boy or a girl. You might even be wallaby twins for all I know at this stage. I read yesterday that couples who want to have a boy should make sure that the man ejaculates after the female orgasm, and that if they want a girl the woman should not have an orgasm at all. If they want a boy the man should wear cotton underpants and dip his testicles into cold water for five minutes every morning and night, and make sure he doesn't ejaculate very often in order to keep his sperm count high, but my problem is that apart from the cotton underpants, which I do wear, I can't really remember all that much about the night you were conceived. I'm pretty sure I didn't do the cold-water dip, but I can't remember how the orgasms were shared out, or when. Anyway, whatever or whoever you are in there, man, woman, beast or duck, I hope you realise what you're putting your mum and me through. Last night she had another dream about you in which you turned into a large steel insect which ate all the biscuits in the cupboard and then stayed in there and wouldn't come out. Oh, sorry about the loud music last night, but since it was my birthday we had a bit of a party – at which your mum couldn't drink or smoke, by the way. We had to tell everyone to go at ten-thirty anyway, because you're making her so tired. I don't mean to put pressure on you so early on, but I hope you're worth it.

P.S. Since you will soon be able to hear what's going on in the outside world, how would you feel about learning a foreign language? I've got an old Linguaphone 'Hablamos Español' tape somewhere which I could dust off and play for you.

THE SEX OF THE CHILD

Something I did not expect was that the sex of our unborn child would be such an important issue. It took me the first five months to get my head round the idea that it was going to be human and probably not a lizard or a piece of furniture. Having, at least partially, appreciated that, it took another few months to come to terms with the fact that since it was to be human, it would most likely be a person. That is to say, have a soul of its own that was neither mine nor Anna's. So to be concerned over whether it would be a boy person or a girl person was, to begin with, completely beyond my capabilities.

The only major row we had during the pregnancy was over this touchy subject. As I saw it, the main thing was to get through the pregnancy and birth with the minimum of stress, and hoping desperately for something you don't end up getting, with the ensuing disappointment, seemed to me to be inviting disaster. We were stuck in an R.D. Laing-type knot: I didn't want her to feel I had a preference in case she felt worried or pressured about the possibility of letting me down; she wanted me to be honest about my true feelings, and was torn between the desire for a girl and the desire to give me the son which she thought that as a man I was secretly hoping for. I came up with something feeble like, 'I might find it easier with a son because I don't have any sisters, so I would know where I was with a boy, but I'd be equally happy with a girl, of course'.

It was classic. In trying to be considerate, people so often end up creating conflict. It's a difficult thing to stick to your true feelings and own up to them. Especially when they may make you seem unpopular, unfashionable or stupid. When Stanley eventually arrived, and was so evidently a boy, I hereby own up to the fact that the words in my head were not, 'Oh, it's a boy, how equally satisfying in a totally nonsexist way', but 'It's a fucking boy! Hoo-fucking-ray! It's male! Like me! I *am* Rambo! I *am* King Kong! Henry VIII eat your heart out! Does anybody want a fight?' Luckily these ridiculous and embarrassing feelings subsided as quickly as they had boiled over, and I returned to being the totally reasonable and irritating New Age carer and sharer that I have made myself into.

These days, with scans, they say it's possible to foretell the sex of your baby from about five months. I know of several people who have seen the scan pictures, seen the little willy and balls, and then had girls. Luckily, since scans came in, the tendency to decorate the nursery in pink for a girl or blue for a boy has become less popular, so people are saved the expense of a re-paint.

The only sure way of predicting the sex of the unborn child is to have an amniocentesis, where they stick a syringe down into the woman's belly and suck up a bit of fluid. The process is not entirely risk-free to the foetus, and so is only carried out when necessary for reasons other than gender prediction. There are, however, numerous theories about predicting the future sex of the baby. Pendulums over the belly, acupressure pulse-taking, noting the shape of the pregnancy (roundish for girls, straight out for boys). As far as I can see, they are all, thank God, as unreliable as anything modern technology has come up with, apart from the depth-charge syringe. It spoils the fun to know.

Nevertheless, trying to control the sex of the unborn child is something people have been obsessed with for centuries. Men wishing to father boys were advised in the eighteenth century to have their left testicle removed, and to make sure that the woman lay on her left side during intercourse. As recently as 1984, *Family Circle* was printing stuff about the different types of intercourse required for the creation of girl or boy babies. Evidently, for a boy you should have intercourse between what the woman believes to be the last low temperature before ovulation, i.e. on the morning on which you note a marked rise in temperature: 'Your best chance of conceiving a boy is when intercourse is timed as close as possible to the shift from peak mucus back to thicker cloudier mucus.' For £39, one can buy a 'Swiss Lady', a sort of wristwatch worn by the woman, which will tell her when it's a better time for her to have intercourse for conceiving boys, and when for girls. Diet is said to be important: if she wants a boy, she should eat lots of meat, fish and eggs, and drink tea, coffee and fizzy drinks; if she wants a girl, milk, cheese, yoghurt, vegetables, and no alcohol. Lady Longford claimed in the *Sunday Telegraph* in November 1991 that she experimented by eating acid foods for boys, and alkali for girls: 'I'm sure it worked.'

Dr Ericsson, from California (obviously) has made a business out of this weakness in people. With his 'sperm isolation technique' he reckons to be able to control with some certainty the sex of a baby. He claims that the sex of a child is determined by the chromosome contained in the sperm, and that male chromosome sperm is more energetic and aggressive than female. There is a Japanese technique for isolating these boy-producing sperms where they strain the semen through a raw egg; any sperm that can get through that has got to be male. In November 1991, Dr Ravi Gupta opened a clinic in England where, for £350, he claims to be able to control the sex of your future child. Dr Ericsson considers this to be the 'ultimate consumer choice'. It's interesting, although shocking, that amniocentesis is banned in some parts of India because parents may be more likely to abort if they know that their child is female.

I can understand and sympathise with couples who have to go through all this temperature-taking and planning in order to conceive at all, but I personally couldn't be bothered to meddle in this way merely to determine gender, even if success were guaranteed, and even though, according to Dr Ericsson, if a man wants a boy he should try for deep penetration at his climax.

Sometimes, no doubt, it must be necessary to interfere, as in certain hereditary diseases, where boys are at risk but not girls, or vice versa, but I'm still amazed that people seriously try to mess about with nature like this for social or political reasons. It's difficult to credit, but the chairperson of the Committee on Human Fertilisation and Embryology, Baroness Warnock, was quoted in the *Sunday Correspondent* on 22 April, 1990 as saying: 'The aristocracy should be allowed to choose the sex of their children to ensure the preservation of male hereditary titles'. Maybe she had been on holiday for three weeks, and thought it was still 1 April.

This all seems even sillier in the light of the work of Ann Moir and David Jessel, who claim in their book *Brain Sex* that it is hormones, not chromosomes, which are most likely to determine the sex of the child. They say that for the first six or seven weeks of pregnancy, the foetus has no gender. Genes do not guarantee the sex of a child. At seven weeks, the mother's body produces massive amounts of hormones. The baby will only develop as a boy if male hormones are present in sufficient enough quantities at this stage. Rather like in adolescence, when kids go all greasy and spotty while their bodies overdose on hormones, except that at seven weeks the amounts are at least four times greater. As it is, after puberty men have twenty times more testosterone in their bodies than women.

They go on to say that all human brains are divided into a right- and a left-hand side, with a sort of multicore joining the two. Early knowledge of this tended to come from the battlefield, however, where most of the brains cut open were male, and so understanding of male/female brain types has been slow in developing. Each side of the brain, it was discovered, is responsible for various areas of ability. In Maryland, in the sixties, Herbert Landfell discovered that men with right-side brain damage did badly in tests relating to spatial skills, but the 'relative performance of similarly brain-damaged women was scarcely affected', meaning that in the female brain, the right/left division is less predominant, and that women's brains are more adaptive. In other words, men's brains are more stringently compartmentalised than women's. In women, language and spatial skills are based in both sides of the brain, but in men such skills are more specifically located. Men's brains are more specialised, more pedantic. One man told by researchers to show more affection to his partner, decided to wash her car.

These days, fashionable parents, or NAPPIES as they are sometimes called (New Age Proud Parents), or even YAPPIES (Young Affluent Parents Who Have Found a New Direction in Life), try so desperately hard to do the right thing that they become very disappointed when, for instance, as happened with friends of mine, their daughter only wants to wear a pink frock and refuses to wear jeans, or when their son runs straight out into the playground, puts his hand up a girl's dress and then smashes her on the nose.

At about four months, all my worryings and caring for Anna are rewarded when at last she has an abnormal food desire. Sardines with pears at midnight. And we've run out! At last I can feel like a proper prospective father. I race out and get the midnight feast. To my surprise and annoyance, no one in the shop says to me, 'Hang on a minute, sardines and pears? At midnight? Are you a prospective father or something?' I have to wake her up to eat them when I get back, as the desire faded while I was out and she nodded off, but at last I can feel useful, or imagine I am in a Walter Matthau film about a harassed prospective father. Unfortunately, the only other strong food desire she has is for massive amounts of the kind of ice cream that nowadays is advertised as if it were a sex aid. I say unfortunately, because we stock up the freezer with tubs of Pecan and Maple, Dutch Double Chocolate, Crunchy Toffee and Devon Cream, and since we spend most evenings in now, I end up eating my share. I start to put on weight almost as rapidly as she does, except mine doesn't look so curvaceous and beatific. No, mine just looks blotchy and middle-aged.

We are walking along the road together one day when a fire engine goes by with a whooping siren. Anna stops dead in the street. 'Baby didn't like that', she says, 'How do you know'? I ask. 'It moved, it kicked me'. The idea of the baby in there is enough to turn my brain to jelly; the idea that it can move about and kick her from inside sends me into a cloud of marshmallow; but the idea that it can actually hear what's going on outside, admittedly through fluid, is enough to make me go completely numb. 'Do you mean we should stop swearing now in case the baby picks up bad habits?' The baby is already there with us, just the other side of her skin. Some people believe you should play soothing classical music against a pregnant woman's stomach to entertain and educate the foetus, to help it grow in a positive and beautiful-person way. That night, I sing 'Amazing Grace', a couple of sea shanties, and a medley of old Beatles hits into Anna's stomach. Over the next few weeks I have moderate success in getting the baby to relax and go to sleep when it's keeping us awake by thrashing around inside Anna late at night. It's favourite song seems to be 'My Way'. Does this mean it's going to spend a lot of time in pubs with pianos when it grows up'?

Later, we can actually see, under the surface, the baby moving around in there. The bulge of a hand, foot or elbow, will roll across Anna's tummy like Jaws under a blanket. To begin with, Anna has to guide my hand to where the movement is, and we have to wait: 'There's one, did you feel it?' But later the baby's kicks are plainly visible. This is inexpressibly exciting. Agonising bliss.

THREE

Dear Foetus,

Would it matter awfully to you if I just buggered off right now and hid somewhere in Iceland for the rest of my life? I've had a think about it and realised that once you arrive, the game will be up, so to speak. Once you know who I am, I'll never be able to leave. Okay, you might not actually recognise me for the first seven months or so after you're born, but the problem is, I suspect, that once you're out and I've clapped eyes on you, I won't feel like going anyway, and so I'll be stuck with you forever, which might be too much for me to cope with. I'm thoroughly daunted by this love thing, and can't imagine me putting your welfare above everything. Yes, it's definitely more sensible for me to bugger off now before you've ever seen the light of day. You'll never know what you're missing then, and will be none the wiser. I know I'm your biological father and all that, but hey, listen, you wouldn't have wanted to get mixed up with someone like me anyway. I'm no good. Really I'm not. People like me don't deserve to have children. Look, I'll call you from Reykjavik, OK? Oh, and could you send me a photo of yourself every now and then? And a cassette recording of your first words would be nice. Don't accept sweets from strangers. Don't go into the entertainment business – it's a mug's game. And never wear light socks with dark shoes. There, that's about it.

STARTING TO WOBBLE

Convinced by a homeopathic doctor, an aunt, several waiters in Italian restaurants and female intuition that we are going to have a girl, we set about thinking of names one night. We go through everything from Arabella to Zeta, and settle on Lilly. All Anna's diary entries at around this time talk of 'Lilly'. Once the name has been agreed, I become overwhelmed with a strange sensation, and cannot sleep. I am propelled into the second bedroom, which will be 'Lilly's' room, by an urge to paint a picture. Somehow, naming the foetus has turned the pregnancy from a physical event to be managed into a person, and this realisation is not so easy to cope with. It seems the most logical thing to do at two in the morning, to get out my old set of paints, unused for years, and paint a picture for 'Our Lilly'. Being considerably out of practice, what I come up with is a nasty splurge of meaningless shapes on a crinkled-up piece of paper and a paintbrush stain on the carpet.

Next morning, I stick the picture on the wall anyway, because it seems to have a significance. Over the next few months, my urge to draw, colour, paint and make stains on the carpet, which has lain dormant since I was eleven, burgeons and blossoms. At five months I go out and buy two enormous sheets of hardboard, primer, some new acrylic paints and a proper brush, find an old saucer to save the carpet from further sploshes, and cover one end of the sitting room in newspaper. Two six-foot by four-foot dot paintings are begun in the style of Aboriginal Papunya paintings, and while Anna rests watching telly, I slowly cover the boards with multi-coloured symbols and shapes. At six months, I buy complicated colouring books and spend my evenings fastidiously filling in with a different colour every jewel on pictures of medieval costumes.

At around seven months, I also start trying to write a story. Unsurprisingly enough, it has a pregnancy in it. It is a reworking of the old changeling myth, where the devilish fairies take a child and put a changeling in its place. The parents have to throw the changeling onto the fire, and the father goes in pursuit of their real child to fairyland. My version is no better than the picture I did for Lilly. It doesn't make sense, and is full of Anna's and my nightmares of giving birth to monster babies who gnash you with pointy teeth, large steel insects who crunch you with their mandibles, and mechanical dogs who travel fast on wheels and bite your ankles. Maybe my intuition is telling me that in fact we don't have a Lilly at all, but a Stanley, and that I will have to go to fairyland to claim him from the devilish fairies, but I doubt it. A more likely explanation is that all these mad and half-arsed stabs at creativity come from the horrible realisation that Anna has a person inside her, not a thing, and that it is she, not I, who is going to give birth to it, and that it is already more important to her than I am.

I write an embarrassingly adolescent poem, something else I haven't done for some years, about how it's as if Anna is the star of some very long-running TV series in which I will be lucky to get a co-producer credit. I can create all the weird symbolic pictures, nonsensical stories and embarrassing poems I like, but I can't create a 'Lilly'. And I can't even really admit that I'm jealous. Of Anna for having a baby, of baby for being more important than me. Of course, once Stanley arrived the need to create all this junk evaporated, because he was there in the flesh, demanding attention and being fun to get to know. But at seven months, there he was in the dark, inside Anna, totally in her domain, totally dependent on her, totally under her control. The idea of never again being the centre of attention was frightening. I slid into the grip of doubts. Did I really want to be a father at all, let alone a good one? Would I have any role in the family after the child was born, other than as Second Assistant

Nappy-Changer? Had this really all gone completely out of control? Should I leave now? If I left, where could I put my two enormous pieces of hardboard?

DO CHILDREN NEED FATHERS?

It used to be unthinkable for a woman to have a child on her own, but nowadays she can decide when she is ready to be a mother, get a teaspoonful of semen from somewhere, and have a child, expecting no further involvement from the father, or indeed any father. We could see this as a positive step towards women taking more control of their own lives, or we could see it as an affront to morality, and dangerous for the children. While this controversy rages, men, understandably, are beginning to feel a teeny-weeny bit edgy about their role in the world. 'You mean a test-tube of that stuff I've been spilling all over the place since I was twelve is all a woman needs from me, forever?'

GENETICS

It's an interesting thought that although I can produce millions of sperms every day, and she can only produce one egg a month, just one of my sperms has as much say in the genetic make-up of our child as does her one egg. Yes, genetically speaking, it's fifty-fifty all the way. It's another example, I suppose, of biology being unfair to the woman. Her investment in creating a new life is hugely greater than the man's: before she's even conceived, let alone after conception, she puts in more in terms of food reserves, and there is also of course the use of her body as incubator and, later, milking machine. In fact, apart from mushrooms and coral, this imbalance is echoed throughout all species. Even in frogs, where neither sex has a penis, the sex cells, or 'gametes', of the male are smaller and more numerous than those of the female, but provide half the genetic information necessary to produce tadpole jelly.

So, since she starts out by investing more than the male in the form of her large food-rich egg, a mother is already at the moment of conception more deeply 'committed' to each child than the father is. Genetically speaking he might as well invest all over the place. Put a different gamete in every port. But that's only genetically speaking, and there are other things to take into consideration, like how expensive that would be in baby buggies and changing-tables. There are all sorts of species which are pair bonded – swans, hedgehogs – and some, like kittiwakes, share equally in the child-rearing. To counteract this imbalance, or even exploitation of the female, all kinds of behaviours have arisen to even out the investment and ensure that the expecting female is not abandoned. Long courtship routines that have to be gone through before the female will copulate, displays of nest-building skills by the male. In the human race, dragon-slaying, muscle-building, motor cycle-driving and making lots of cash are popular, and more recently, pram-pushing, caring, sharing, bonding, cake-making, being able to cry, and talking about feelings.

NEW MAN

'When we got pregnant, we thought, we don't know anything about babies, or children, we'd better go and have a look at some, and we nearly got arrested peering through the wire at a load of toddlers in a playground.' This was actually a woman talking, but these days one hears both men and women discussing pregnancy as a joint activity. 'When we got pregnant . . .', 'When we gave birth to our first baby . . .'.

Men can and do go through sympathetic pregnancy with their wives. It's called couvade. I read somewhere that in certain tribes in New Guinea they take their couvade very seriously indeed. When a woman goes into labour, her husband will go through tortured agony on her behalf and develop any number of symptoms, working himself up into a frenzy. After the birth, he recovers, and his friends are as likely to come up to him to ask how the labour went as they are his wife. 'How was it?' 'Oh, you wouldn't believe it, fourteen hours of sheer hell. In the end they had to give me a Caesarean. Fancy a pint?' Apart from the obvious benefits derived by the men from the formalising of this couvade into a ceremony – it gives them something to do – it is believed that the pain suffered by the man in this ritual actually reduces his wife's during labour. Maybe we should incorporate it into our way of life in the West, so that expectant mothers could be offered alternatives to the usual painkillers, gas, air and water birth, etc. 'Oh I won't be needing the epidural, thank you, my husband's having a heart attack instead.' Of course, couvade does happen over here, and there are frequent cases of expectant fathers falling ill as their wives go into labour, suffering from attacks that are not always imagined. There is definitely a lot of incomprehensible magic around from the moment of conception. However, I don't think I would have been much use to Anna if I'd had a hysterical choking fit right through her labour. It's questionable, though, whether I was any use standing by her side reminding her to breathe, something which, let's face it, she wouldn't have forgotten for very long anyway.

FEELING LEFT OUT

But how important is the father, really? Could the human race get on better without him? Have instead a sperm bank where prospective mothers can choose genetic cocktails while the few remaining males in the world are kept safely on a male reservation where they can drink, kick balls around, fight, fart and play with the train sets as much as they like?

Until recently, I believed what I'd been told, that all men are the same, and are only interested in one thing. 'In days of old when knights were bold and women weren't invented, they used to drill holes in telegraph poles to keep themselves contented', ran an old playground rhyme. But now I'm not so sure. Oh no! I'm not turning into a 'New Man' am I? How embarrassing.

The concept of the New Man is not actually very new. The phrase 'new man' appeared in *The Times* in 1891. In 1921, Floyd Dell and his friends Max Eastman and Hutchins Hapgood were writing articles such as 'Feminism for Men' in their magazine *The Masses*, which apparently stood for 'Fun, Truth, Beauty, Realism, Freedom, Peace, Feminism, and Revolution'. They believed that 'the bravest thing will not be done in the world until women do not have to look to men for support'. Like so many well-intentioned idealists they worked their way through several women and wives each, and seemed to have gone more for 'Fun' and 'Beauty' than 'Realism' and 'Truth'. Whether they were there when their children had chickenpox, or even paid maintenance, I haven't been able to find out.

The trouble is, men so desperately want to be important. And it comes quite hard to realise that in the rather major area of childbirth, they're not, or at least not central to the issue. You can bicker away in the divorce courts about who owned the Led Zeppelin albums, or whether the teapot was a present from his mother or hers, but in the end all that matters are 'the best interests of the child'.

There is a feeling of displacement and uselessness at being the one who doesn't have the baby, at being the one without the innate cuddling-caring skills, that deprives some men of meaning to their lives, and which might explain the number of absentee fathers. The important child psychologist D. W. Winnicott concluded in his book *The Child, the Family and the Outside World* that the greatest thing a father can do for his children in the early years is 'to be alive and stay alive', which doesn't sound very important compared to what the mother has to go through. Needless to say, the chapter about the father is very late on in Winnicott's book, and is much slimmer than the others.

It has now become a cliché to remind mothers that if they want to have the father around, they must allow him into the care of the baby as more than just an assistant. This means not readjusting every Pamper he sticks on crooked, and not rechanging the baby every time he has dressed it in an unsatisfactory colour scheme. In the same way that men have had to adjust to women with power in the workplace, women have had to allow their partners 'sole care' of the baby more often, and to relinquish some of their God-given right to control in the nursery. And in my experience, women are as egotistical in this area as men are when it comes to cars and sport. To call a women a bad mother is still the nastiest knife you can cut her with. Yes, women have their equivalent of the medallion man, and are just as competitive as men, but about different things. 'Oh, I was in labour for seventy-nine hours, and I didn't need any painkillers at all . . .' and 'Oh, did you only breast-feed for three years'? are both examples of what I call 'Facho'.

So here I am, the initiate New Age man, an eager puppy, talking about babies in the pub and dithering around dying for a drink at home, discovering what women have no doubt known for ages, that success in life depends not on being single-minded, but on coping with dilemmas, on muddling through, on damage limitation. My first major dilemma came as soon as we had booked the predicted arrival day at the hospital. I was offered a stonking great job that would take me abroad for eight weeks directly after the birth, and if the birth were a few days late, would mean missing the whole thing entirely. Having just spent hundreds of pounds on changing-tables, cots, buggies, nappies and assorted baby gear, we needed the money, and obviously we were going to need money still more after the baby arrived. The choice was not just a simple one between old chauvinist man unfeelingly running off to pursue his career, and new dungaree-clad home-husband staying close to the family to care and share. No, at that point, staying at home could have meant caring for a very hungry wife and child, and having nothing but second mortgages, debts and resentment to share with them. Going, however, would have meant caring only in the chequebook sense. A proper dilemma, and a great test for what the rest of our lives was going to be like. As with all such problems, the solution was not to be spectacular and decisive. I managed to find another, smaller job in radio, far less well paid, but it meant I could stay around. It was also a very time-consuming one, which meant I got

47

hardly any sleep. Another good preparation for what was to come.

The commonest cause of divorce is the arrival of children. The family income can be halved at a stroke when the mother gives up work, so the father is likely to work overtime in response. Being locked out of the intimacy a mother shares with her new child, typical male reactions have been to work more, become obsessed with a hobby, find another woman, or get pissed. Typical male reactions to being invited to share that intimacy and the responsibility that goes with it, have been to whinge more, become obsessive or violent, compete with the mother to be better at it, or get pissed.

ABSENTEE

John Boorman's film *Emerald Forest* is the true story of a boy who at the age of seven was taken from his parents by rainforest Indians and brought up by them. The film follows the ten-year quest of the real father to find his son. When they are reunited, the boy has no conscious memory of his first family, but, in true Boorman style, he rekindles his subconscious memory of them through the use of his newly acquired skill in magic, and the help of Indian hallucinogenic drugs. It may seem far-fetched that a seventeen-year-old could have obliterated all memories of the first seven years of his life from his conscious mind, but, as Boorman explains in his book about the film, *Money into Light*, this part of the story was fully researched and in line with the events of the actual lives on which the film was based.

After seven, evidently, the memory becomes more tenacious. Of course, it's also true that traumas, like being snatched away from your parents, tend to sink to the bottom of the subconscious, but nevertheless, it makes one think, doesn't it, 'what's the point?' If you have to wait seven years before the ungrateful little bastard even remembers who you are, is it worth it? All those sleepless nights and food-spattered floors, and then by the time he does know who you are, he'll just think you're a stupid old fart anyway. And, come to think of it, it'll probably be a good seven years before your partner even notices your presence again, she's so preoccupied with the little sod. And as for sex . . . . Well, despite those careful line drawings in the small 'And the Father' chapter in all the pregnancy books, where the bloke always seems to have a beard out of ABBA, and the couple seem to be doing something that looks more like a sequence from a Buddhist meditation video than any serious shagging, sex now seems to have lost some of its pzazz.

'I'm just off to buy a packet of cigarettes and a newspaper, darling.' and out of the door you go for ever, often leaving a note that says something to the effect of: 'I just didn't feel needed any more', to which, if she can ever find you, you'll get the reply: 'Good riddance. Now where's the money?'

who's sleeping in my bed

FOUR

Dear Creature from the Amniotic Lagoon

Hurry up. We're both totally bored with this waiting game. You've completely immobilised your mum, and she just wants to get on with it now. So do I. The anticipation is killing us. Surely you must have had long enough drinking the soup of life in there by now? Get on with it. Can't you engage your head, or break her waters or something? By the way, let me apologise in advance that we didn't manage to arrange for a totally natural birth with water, Vivaldi and Buddhist chanting, but the place they do that is right over the other side of town, and with the traffic these days, if you did decide it was time and were in a hurry to come out, your first view of the world would be of the roadworks at Paddington from the back seat of a Fiat Uno. Also, sorry that it's only London and not the Caribbean or the South of France. Don't expect any good weather. And it will be September, so you've got a winter ahead of you. But apart from that, I'm sure you'll be fine. You've got a squishy skull, so getting out shouldn't be too bad. I'll explain the rest when you get here.

ANTENATAL CLASS

'And to bath a baby, you always support its head, like so.'
  'Whaaaaa!'
'Test the water with your elbow, like so.'
  'Whaaaaa!'
Everything else the midwife says is completely drowned out by the unbelievable decibel level coming from the tiny little maggot of a baby that she is, very professionally, holding. She soldiers on, ignoring the din. How can so much noise come from such a small creature? Its mother sits a couple of feet away in a hospital dressing gown, looking absolutely, completely and utterly knackered. Both mother and baby have on plastic hospital wrist-tags. The baby is only a few days old. I shift uncomfortably on my chair. It is a metal chair, and the sound of scraping on the floor joins the general commotion in this very large, echoing room at the Queen Charlotte's Hospital. It is men's night on the antenatal course, and about fifteen of us have turned up to learn how to bath baby and how not to take it personally if our partners become irritable, depressed or downright aggressive towards us in the weeks after childbirth.

Men over twenty or so are not used to domestic science classes. The times they meet as a gender group are usually to do with work, alcohol or sport, and none of us even knows how to sit comfortably in this situation, let alone feed, change or bath a baby. The presence of a real baby and its mother adds to the discomfort. I feel embarrassed, as if we are intruding on something very private. The poor woman who agreed to have her baby used for the demonstration is sitting like a beached whale, her eyes glazed over. It is her baby's first bath, and, we are told, she doesn't know how to bath it either. This makes it even worse. In actual fact, she is most likely blissfully happy sitting there, showing off her beautiful creation to fifteen pairs of male eyes. We are the ones shifting in our chairs, trying to look as if we aren't scared.

We are a very eclectic bunch. Men of all shapes and sizes, all classes and capabilities. The only thing we have in common, apart from our maleness, is the fact that we have gone and got a woman pregnant and didn't take the first boat to Australia on hearing the news. There is a man dressed entirely in black who sits by the open window glowering and smoking (except when the baby is brought in, of course). There is one who looks like a stunt man from *Minder* , with chunky gold jewellery and a fake Rolex, who pretends to be more stupid than he is in order to preserve his masculinity. 'Could you just explain that bit again, darling? You'll have to spell it out, love, for someone like me, 'cos I don't know nothing about all this,' followed by a leery grin round the room for approval. There is an Indian businessman who nods in silence, and a guy in a leather jacket who doesn't look old enough to have left school yet. There is a suited and flat-briefcased yuppie who announces proudly at the beginning of the session that he is going to switch his mobile phone into off-mode for a whole hour. Also no doubt expecting general approval, and possibly a small round of applause. There is a wild, unshaven, grey-haired man of about sixty, in open sandals, who is working his way through the hospital biscuits provided with the tea at the halfway break. And there is a massively tall, bearded, bespectacled geography teacher of a man who has with him an enormous hardbacked notebook in which he writes down everything the midwife says with one of his five ballpoint pens. He has geography-teacher sensible shoes, tweed jacket and corduroy trousers. He also has a geography-teacher voice. Very loud, strident, and 'playgroundy', 'Could I just confirm', he booms, 'whether the second stage of labour can be reached without the breaking of the water, or is it that in *every case* the mucus plug must come out for this stage to proceed?' He carefully writes down every answer, and then looks obsessively through the notes he made before this evening to see if he can find another really fiddly question to test out on the midwife. Maybe he isn't a prospective dad at all. Maybe he's hoping to go on *Mastermind*, with childbirth as his special subject.

I look around the group. What a sorry lot we are. I pity the fifteen sprogs who are going to be born to this bunch of frightened little boys. And I include myself. Really, after how many million years, is this the best the human race can do in the way of fathers for its little ones? Or will having kids turn us all magically and instantly into Marcello Mastroianni lookalikes, confident of our masculinity, chunky and authoritative, with sexy Italian accents? Like the wild man, I seem to have eaten more than my share of hospital biscuits. And I'm on my fourth cup of tea. The baby being bathed looks so very, very small. The responsibility of having something as helpless as that to care for seems almost obscene in its awesomeness. Have another biscuit. At this moment, I feel like a character in a Tom and Jerry cartoon, when they have run out three feet past the edge of the cliff, but have not yet started to plummet downwards. There is always that little second in midair, when they realise they have overshot the cliff, before their arms and legs start to helicopter round and they whizz down to get flattened or turned into dust. I hope that when I get down there, I have a cartoon character's power to reform myself and pop back into shape.

Is it normal for men to become so involved in the birth of children I ask myself. And at what point does involvement become interference? It has been taboo for many thousands of years. Did people in earlier times know something we've forgotten? Paula Yates, the wife of Bob Geldof, often sounds off in public about how little Bob does in the way of nappy-changing etc. Not in a nasty or malicious way, she just says he's squeamish; so he doesn't do it, fair enough. Do women in fact need to have something to complain about in a man? That would be a relief. I can think of plenty of things I do that would satisfy. What am I doing here? What happens if I get really, really good at supporting the baby's head and testing its water with my elbow? What if I get better at it than Anna? How will she feel? I can feel a sitcom with Peter Bowles and Penelope Keith coming on. *Some Fathers Do 'Ave 'Em.*

Just in time, the screaming baby is taken out of the room by its tired mum, and the evening is over. A few, rather pathetic jokes are cracked among us, and we file out into the night. On my way home, I am more aware than ever of the pressure on men these days to prove themselves in the feelings/crying/household departments. It is quite confidence-sapping. This must be rather what it's like for women reading magazines like *Cosmopolitan*, with their streams of articles about 'How to get your man', 'How to get rid of your man', 'How to get promotion without upsetting your man', 'How to upset your man without getting promotion'. They must be as sick of being told that 'Today's girl knows what she wants, and isn't afraid to go out and get it', as I am beginning to

I don't need a bath

get of hearing that as a man I don't know how to express my feelings. A man who builds a monstrous tower block or designs a vicious warplane may not be a very nice chap, but he's sure as hell expressing his feelings.

BIRTH

Anna's contractions started three days early, after Sunday lunch at her mum's. We went home at six and rang the hospital at seven, and then again at nine. It was important to make sure it wasn't a false alarm and in any case, her waters hadn't broken, so we were told to wait until the gaps between the contractions became considerably shorter. It was extraordinarily soothing to be in the grip of such a powerful rhythm. Like the tide coming in. She knelt against the bed, breathing slow and deep. So calm, and so concentrated, she seemed like a diver preparing for a complicated high dive.

In these few hours before the contractions accelerate, life becomes like a Pinter play. Conversation becomes weird and disjointed. Less is said – but the pauses! Whoever invented the phrase 'pregnant pause' knew what they were talking about.

'You want salad . . .?'

'Yes . . .'

'Now . . .?'

'Maybe . . .'

'In the sitting room or . . .?'

'No, just a bowl with a spoon . . .'

'It's 9.55 . . .'

'. . . What's the time?'

'We'll ring the hospital again at five-past ten . . .'

'. . . Is it getting shorter since the last contraction?'

(Pause)

'You're doing really well . . .'

'I'll have my salad after the next one . . .'

And on and on for a delicious few hours in which time

is suspended. No heightened emotions now. We're on a plateau. You could hit me with a saucepan now and I wouldn't feel a thing. You could tell me Spielberg was on the phone with the offer of a major role, and I wouldn't remember his name. For the first time in my life, I'm truly happy pottering about the kitchen, tidying up. It's like a psychedelic track from an early Pink Floyd record. 'Clingfilm? Will we need clingfilm? I'll just put some on the leftover salad . . . We might need it when we get back . . . next century . . .' Faint Hammond organ music revolves like a gentle merry-go-round somewhere in my mind, almost out of earshot. Twinky-twanky George Harrison-type sitar music is weaving sticky cartoon webs between us . . . Timeless cosmic trapeze artists are swooping huge loops and laughing as we check our sponge bags and watches. We are about to be initiated into the human race. I feel like Yul Brynner in some sixties Technicolour epic about Aztecs or Vikings. My comfortable trousers are the multicoloured feather robes Tony Curtis wore in *The Kingdoms of the Sun*, and I've got the same blank, zombie-like expression on my face as he has before the big human sacrifice scene.

The serenity of something really serious, something big and deep, descends on us as we go down in the lift, get into the car, and drive round Hammersmith Broadway at four miles an hour, about the speed of the sedan chair in the huge ceremonial scene in *Cleopatra*. Like anyone encountering a situation loaded with gravity, we make small jokes and small talk . . . 'Why do little ducks walk softly? Because they can't walk hardly.' 'Oh look, that chip shop on Hammersmith Grove has closed down . . .' Despite all the reassuring talk from doctors, relatives and baby books, the statistics in newspapers, the modern programmes about child-rearing, the amazing inter-uterine photography and the old clichés about women who can just squat behind a bush, drop one, chew off the umbilical cord and carry on working in the field, despite all this, we have our unspoken fears, our memories of Victorian novels, of snippets from folklore about women who have died in childbirth, about babies who never make it through the uterine canal, and our complete inability to understand what that would mean to us.

Needless to say, when I consulted Anna about these final few hours whilst writing this, her memory was entirely different. All she could remember was sitting on the toilet because she had to pee so often, and counting the seconds between contractions. And the salad, well, she forgot I even made one. . . . Fair enough, I suppose.

It is now midnight. In the hospital we are put in a curtained booth and told to wait for what seems like ages. Well, it is ages. An hour or two. A couple of uniformed people drop by and disappear again. A form is filled in. We are asked for our 'birthplan', but we don't have one. We had both been against the idea of writing down a schedule for how we felt the birth should go. I know it's a sensible idea from the hospital's point of view, so that they know in advance what they can and can't do. It just seemed such an impossible concept to us, to write out in advance what we intended to happen when embarking on an event that was bound to be nine parts magic.

Finally we are taken to the birthing room. Much anticipation, but we are left alone again. As soon as the midwife appears, to be with Anna, I slope off to the gents for a cigarette. Something which is repeated through the night. Whenever she is not alone, or things seem to be going OK, I sneak out for a quick nicotine fix. But those moments in the gents are not just about tobacco, there's something more personal about them. If I wasn't a fag junkie, I'd miss those few minutes of quiet and solitude. I'd feel stupid saying, 'I'm just going to the toilet again to be with myself for a few seconds'. Too Californian. For the meantime, I'll stick to cigarette addiction.

The story goes that the first time a woman delivered

her baby on her back with her legs up in the air in stirrups, it was at the insistence of Louis XIV, the guy who used to have an audience of a hundred or so fans just to watch him get up and get dressed of a morning. Evidently he decided he wanted to see his child being born, but couldn't be bothered to bend down to look between his wife's legs, so he had her laid out on the bed, while he presumably sat in a big chair a few feet away, fiddling with his remote control. Before that time, it was squatting. Babies sort of fell out downwards, not completely without effort and pain, just in a different direction. After Louis, the new position caught on, like eating cake, and no amount of French Revolutions or Chartist movements changed it until the present day, or at least until the sixties.

The reason the lying-back position has been so prevalent since Louis' day is, we are told, because it is more convenient for the doctors, who are all men. But this doesn't really take into account the work of the midwives, who seem to carry out most of the business. Having done a brief survey of all the people I know, I am none the wiser about which is the 'Right Way'. For instance, one woman had a water birth in a pool in her living room with no complications and a short labour; another began a water birth at a London hospital where they have a pool, but had to be hauled out because there were specks of meconium (little babies' poo) in the water, which evidently meant there was a danger of the baby choking. There then followed a thirty-six-hour labour with Pethidine painkillers, a suction pump and the works. One woman had two babies the old-fashioned way, i.e. lying down with drugs, but for her third thought she would try natural squatting and no painkillers, with dimmed light and soft music instead. After twenty hours or so of complete agony, she gave birth to an enormous eleven-pound baby, having screamed for painkillers, gas, air and even death – to which the natural-birthers around her had replied 'That's not the way we do it here, dear'. Her first word on coming round was 'Vasectomy'.

The most important thing is that a woman should not feel disappointed in herself, or feel in any way a failure because of the method she has chosen, or indeed fallen into. There is such pressure on women to be 'the best' at giving birth. Yes, the experience of being born is the first major trauma for the baby, and how it happens will be with him for the rest of his life, but there is sometimes a tendency for mothers to set themselves goals of perfection that only cause guilt and disappointment if they are not achieved.

The most sensible plan for a birth, I think, is to do whatever causes least anxiety to the mother, be it drugs, warm water or squatting behind a bush. This is not just a question of being nice. Anxiety produces chemicals in the body that are capable of inhibiting or delaying the birth. Her emotional state is therefore in control of events. This also goes for the argument over whether or not the father should be present at the birth. It depends entirely on the individuals. His presence may have a calming effect on his partner, or he may, as Desmond Morris points out in his book *Babywatching*, 'be even more anxious than the mother and risk transmitting his fears to her'.

One man I know, a keen tap-dancer, thought he would get some practice in on the hospital's lovely shiny corridor floor, while waiting for his wife's third stage of labour to begin. The only words she said to him throughout the birth were screamed: 'Stop fucking tap-dancing, you bastard'. What is a chap supposed to do? He can't work the bleep machines, he can't actually do any of the pushing himself, so if she has become bored of holding hands and reassuring whispers in the ear, why not get in a bit of tap practice? But then it's her day, not yours.

Of course, Anna and I had discussed whether I was to be present at the birth, and decided that I would be. It was something Anna had been sure about from the beginning. Even so, I was prepared to have her suddenly scream at me that I should leave. I certainly hadn't bought unquestioningly the idea that the father should be present. It seemed to me that for two thousand years and more, men have not been invited in on this most special moment, and although I agree that for two thousand years the human race has not exactly been getting it right in most areas, I felt there may have been some reason currently obscure, or unavailable to me, why husbands and fathers have hitherto been excluded from the actual moment of birth. One problem, of course, with missing the birth and arriving after it's all over with flowers, is that the well-intentioned New Age father is in danger of bonding with the afterbirth.

Whatever the preamble, whatever the doubts I may have had, I was present right through until five past five, when Stanley was born, and stayed present until eleven o'clock the next morning, when I went home to pick up the salad in clingfilm to bring it back to the hospital. (You scc, I knew we'd need it.) And whatever the rights or wrongs of it, in retrospect I am grateful to Anna and the staff at Queen Charlotte's for having so generously made this possible.

At about 1 a.m., however, I wasn't so sure, as I watched the midwives wire Anna up to the bleeps: little sensory microphones stuck on to her belly to monitor the baby's heartbeat. They are a wonderful invention, but for the next four hours every time she shifted on the bed or rumbled around, the Velcro attaching them would work loose and the signal would become faint or stop. While four professional people concerned themselves with the serious business of bringing Stanley into the world, it was left up to me as the only unnecessary person there to worry about the bleeps. Every now and then, I would notice that a bleep had been missed, inwardly panic, and take a midwife to one side and ask her about it, and she would confidently readjust the Velcro. I did feel like a spare prick.

For some reason, no amount of blood and gore that night made me queasy. No amount of pain (other people's that is) or drama made me wince. The only thing that made me go all wobbly was the epidural. Anna didn't really want to have an epidural, and she was doing fine breathing through the contractions, but there came a point where they convinced us both that she might as well have one put in in case she wanted it later, when it would be too late to rig it up. They said that with it in, she wouldn't have to use it if she didn't want to. What neither of us realised was that putting it in and setting it up are the gruelling parts. With an epidural, they cut a little nick in the skin at the base of the spine and stick in a flexi-syringe. They can then shove painkiller up your spine as much as they like. The advantage is that unlike oral painkillers, the drug does not waft across the bloodstream and get the baby stoned as well.

What we also didn't know was that once it's in, they have to monitor and control your heart rate and body temperature with another little needle shoved in a vein on your wrist. The technology became frightening as Anna went blue and shivery at the flick of a switch. There's something nasty about the feeling of being completely at the control of a machine. I didn't like this bit. I didn't like it at all. Oh why didn't we make a birthplan? Something with 'blue and shivery' crossed out.

I am holding Anna's hand now, trying to be reassuring, but I've gone white and sweaty and am gulping air. I'm leaning on her. Luckily her temperature returns to normal, and, feeling more comfortable, she can move about a bit on the bed. Luckily I don't faint – that would be humiliating. She can actually have a bit of a rest now from the pain of the contractions, which have been going on since lunch at her mum's, and a rest is good, explain the midwives, because she'll need all her strength for what is to come.

At God knows when, Stanley was ready to come out, and the pushing began in earnest. I was allowed to be one of the people Anna used as leverage, pressing her foot up against my hip. It took a while. I don't know how long. There are three stages of labour, and you can read about them in the pregnancy books, or watch someone's New Age video, or a TV documentary. We didn't have a video, or a camera, or even a notebook, thank God, so this is pure, biased recall.

The really difficult bit was getting the head out. It's much wider than the body, and all pointy because it's been squished into an oval shape coming through the uterine canal. The bones are still soft, you see. After the head, the body just seemed to slither out in one go. And it was blue. Cheesy, smelly, blue. Except for an enormous red scrotum and willy. Like a baboon's arse. Bright, bright red. A tiny slithery blue baby, with the cock and balls of a rock star gorilla on heat. Bloody hell, he was a boy all right. I don't know whether I was more surprised to find that our expected 'Lilly' was a boy or by the birth itself.

It was five-past five a.m., and they wiped him down a bit. I am ashamed to say that I can't remember whether they let him lie for a while on Anna's belly before they cut his umbilical cord, by separating off a section of it with tongs. There may have been blood everywhere. I didn't notice anything but him. They sucked the mucus out of his nose and throat with a tube, put a metal clip on his tummy button, and thrust him into my arms. He cried a little, but not excessively. He didn't seem to be too upset about having arrived. He had handled it pretty well. I had not been expecting to have him shoved into my arms so soon. I thought there would be other things that needed doing. I felt guilty that it was me holding him, not Anna, but she was still working, delivering the afterbirth, and they were all attending to her, so she didn't seem ready to take him. I held him at the side of the room while the work went on. I held him close to my stomach. As near to what he was used to as possible. So small. I don't know what I said. 'There, there' probably,

or a few refrains of 'Amazing Grace' or even 'Tiger Feet'
to soothe him. I have no idea what I did, other than stand
there holding him. It seemed unfair that after all Anna
had been through,. I had him.

I've asked several men who've been through this what
their very first thought was, and apart from the usual, 'Is
the baby all right? All there?', they range from 'Bloody
hell, his scrotum's bigger than mine', and 'For the first
time in my life, someone's more important than me', to
'Oh my God, what have I done?' My very first thought
was, 'Oh there you are'. A most unexpected feeling took
hold of me. That I had known him all along, even before
my life began. His face looked as old as the hills. A recog-
nisable landscape locked until this moment in the other
nine-tenths of my brain. Not only had I known him all
along, he had been there all along, through my childhood, my adolescence, my twenties. For this moment,
time was folded in on itself, and there was no difference

between this new life and my great-great-grandfather. If there had been a Buddhist priest present, I would have converted on the spot, so great was the sudden insight into the concept of reincarnation. 'Oh, there you are, of course, how stupid of me to think it would be otherwise. You haven't come from the moon, or another galaxy, you are made of blood and water, the same as everyone else. And all of that's come from what was here on earth in the first place'. He could have had a stamp on him saying, 'This baby is made from recycled humans'.

Eventually (probably only a matter of seconds), I passed him to Anna, we kissed and hugged and cried, and he was put in a dish to be weighed and labelled. I went over to check his label: 'Yes, right name (the mother's) . . . and the label couldn't come off. I didn't want this turning into a 1960s Jack Lemmon movie about swapped babies. Pathetic I know, but nerves were jangled.

Baby and mother are shoved on a trolley and we're whirled through the hospital. As we bounce into the wide lift, I'm looking at Anna in sweaty admiration. She must be the most brilliant woman God ever created. All women in one. An athlete, psychologist, earth mother, sex beast; big-breasted, bloody, organic and terrifying. She looks knackered, and so delicate, and so satisfied.

I wake up on her bed. I was meant to be listening out in case she has difficulty taking her first wee-wee, but must have nodded off. I wake up again on the hospital floor. I go and check the baby room where they have taken Stanley to let Anna get some sleep. A little bit later on, he is beside her bed, asleep in a long see-through plastic box, and I sit and look at him while she rests. He's on his side, wrapped up with just his face poking out. He still looks ancient, but he's no longer blue. He's beetroot. One job a man is meant to do is to remember to bring lots of 10 pences and the address book so that he can telephone friends and relatives. I have a phonecard as well, just in case. I must have done it, but I can't remember when. Nine-thirty the next day maybe. People come to visit, there are flowers, and soft toys, and snaps are taken. People say, 'Isn't he beautiful? Isn't he lovely?' and are right.

I slept, I woke, sometimes in a chair, sometimes on my own in the flat. I visited every few hours. I don't know how many days went by, maybe two or three. For the first few days, the mother's breasts don't give out milk, but a sort of transparent antibiotic goo called colostrum. And what comes out of the baby's bottom is not like poo, but is meconium, a sort of greeny-black treacle that smells absolutely wonderful. Everything about babies smells wonderful. Especially their scalps. It's only later, when they turn into sweaty, mucky toddlers that they start to get that yucky stench you recognise the moment you walk into a school.

As I gradually descended to earth over the next few days, I realised that the flat was in no way ready to welcome a new mother and child. The room we had set aside for 'Lilly' – previously my office – was still curtainless, and had unsanded Polyfilla all over the walls. Every moment not working or in the hospital, was spent painting and decorating and buying things like those bedside lamps that look like ducks. It was one thing to be by her side bringing him into the world, but quite another to realise what I should have been doing all along, which was to feather the nest so we could return home as a family.

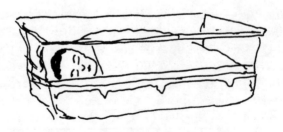

FIVE

October 1988

Dear Nameless One, or one who shall remain nameless until we can agree on something,

I am lost for words. Is this what it was all for? Is this what life is really all about? I've got to get a sense of proportion... If you think of the earth as about the size of a party balloon, then the moon would be a small ping-pong ball about seventy football pitches away, and the sun, well, that would be the size of a few cathedrals several thousand miles further off still. So that's how important we all are. So why can't I shake off this feeling that you are, in fact, incredibly significant?

Then again, if I were to think of each molecule in your brain as being about the size of a ping-pong ball, then your fluffy penguin mobile would be hundreds of football pitches away, and your mum would eclipse the sun completely.

Who would have though that this is the kind of crazy stuff going on in my mind, as to all outward appearances my time is completely taken up with negotiating the obstacle course which the flat has become? There isn't a square inch left that is not being used to house some piece of baby-care equipment or other.

In the short gaps when you are sleeping, instead of grabbing a few minutes' kip like sensible people would, we tend to creep up and gaze at you, ostensibly to check that you are comfortable and surviving, but really just to gloat with pride.

WASHING MACHINE FIASCO

When I was in my early twenties, washing machines used to be things that stood in rows, with bent coin slots sticking out of them like tongues at the doctor when you have a sore throat. When I hit thirty and moved into my own flat, the previous owners had left their washing machine behind, along with the broken fridge, the blackened electric cooker and the extractor fan covered in the sort of gunk that looks like peanut butter made from charcoal. This inherited washing machine, while not being exactly a model of efficiency, had great character, and I got on quite well with it for some years. Once a week, it would be required to uo two washes – one whites, one coloureds – for which it would summon up fantastic amounts of energy. At 'spin' it would become comically overexcited and start walking out into the middle of the room, making a noise like a World War One biplane trying to take off. I had to stay nearby to coax it back into its alcove, in case it tugged itself from its bindings, scurried into the middle of the room and, tearing its connection to the hot-water pipes, flooded the kitchen and the kitchens of people as far as three floors below. Often, clothes would come out covered in little white clumps of congealed washing powder and smelling like a vegetable market at the end of the day. For drying, I had one of those foldable mini climbing frames which collapse into the bath when your back is turned so that the leaking bath tap can give everything a final rinse while you're asleep or out at work.

This blissful domestic way of life had carried on unnoticed, as I say, for several years, until the arrival of Stanley. Unnoticed, at any rate, by myself. I'm sure Stanley's mum, had I bothered to ask, would have been able to predict what the arrival of a child would mean for the future of my cosy relationship with the ancient but enthusiastic washing machine. Not being the sort of woman who fancies carrying laundry down to the river every day and beating it on the rocks for several hours to get it clean, she politely suggested that we update our antiquated clothes-cleaning operations. In other words, got a new washing machine. I was horrified, and as you can imagine, resisted this heresy for as long as I could. One week.

Although a baby's clothes are much smaller than ours, they get through them at about seven times the speed. For decades, I have been accustomed to a clean pair of socks and underpants per day, which means seven sets a week. No problem. A baby can get through that in a morning and still have some dribble or sick left over to smear down your lapel. Getting a meal into a baby's mouth and not on the furniture, carpet, your clothes, or his, is a task as hard to master as monocyling. Oh, you can cover everything in plastic, and put saucepans and buckets all over the floor to catch flying pellets of oats and apple slop, but the baby will always be cleverer than you and find a chink in your armour. For every mouthful that goes in baby, five will end up where you don't want them: down his vest, in his hair, in yours, up his sleeve, in your shoe and, later, if hands have not been properly wiped, smeared on the windows, the sheets and, worst of all, on the pile of clean clothes waiting to be ironed.

My poor old washing machine slipped its drum after a few days of this new workload. And as for drying, there were so many damp clothes draped everywhere that the flat began to look like the inside of a whole earth meditation marquee. A washing machine, and a dryer, were required, and fast. After tearful goodbyes, we got rid of my tired old friend and installed two average new machines made by an average company which shall remain nameless. Nameless, because there then followed possibly the most stressful two months of my life. Just because you have paid a fair amount of money for something, there is no guarantee that it will actually work.

Just because you have a five-year warranty on something, that doesn't mean it's not going to break down again and again, or that anyone from the insurers, the manufacturer or the shop from which it came, will answer the phone, or accept responsibility if they do. If someone is coming to fix it, they will not be able to tell you when, so you have the choice between giving up your job, social life, shopping or anything else, to wait in in case they bother to turn up, invariably without the required spare part; taking the machine apart yourself (not advisable, as you lose all guarantees and flood the kitchen); kicking the machine in a blind fury (likewise); or having a nervous breakdown.

I opted for the last of these. While Anna did the constant runs to the launderette we now required, I stayed at home with the baby and the phone, because, we rationalised, I have a better phone manner, and she wanted to get out of the flat for a bit anyway. In fact, my phone manner quickly became abusive and desperate and thus totally ineffective. Coping with a screaming baby, a wet kitchen, a pile of soggy, half-clean clothes, and indifferent voices on the end of the phone, was not what I felt my life was meant to be about, and often Anna would come back to a husband having a worse tantrum than any two-year-old could manage. I made a complete mess of it. Once, I threatened a sales person that I would arrive at the shop with the baby and the dirty washing, and harangue all their customers like a deranged weirdo from Speakers' Corner; 'Don't buy washing machines from this shop or you'll end up like me!' After being convinced by various friends that this would probably be a rather stupid thing to do, we sent back the new washing machines, splashed out a ludicrous amount of money, and bought the state-of-the-art machines that we still have today. These machines make about as much noise as the London traffic does if you live in Cornwall. At 'spin' they don't even jiggle around, let alone walk into the centre of the room. If you could work out all of their

70

functions, they could probably sew on buttons and take up trousers. For our purposes, however, they are like using a word processor with spread sheet, modem and database as a mere typewriter, but our clothes are clean, and the only person I have to argue with on the phone now is my bank manager, who, understandably, wanted me to take out a second mortgage to pay for them

I still give these two machines a scowl every time I walk past them, because they represent a giving-in. They remind me of my inability to cope, and as they sit there, smugly doing the business, each barely discernible pro-gramme–changing click they make whispers evilly to my conscience: 'You'll be getting a Volvo next, and finding *Joint Account* funny, and then who knows? Voting Con-servative. . . Where will this all end? Eh?' Of course I know that buying a state-of-the-art washing machine and dryer doesn't necessarily mean that one should be completely written off in the young, wild and irresponsi-ble stakes, but it did seem to me at the time to be the thin end of the middle-aged wedge. Immediately you have a child, society seems to take great pleasure in say-ing, 'Aha! Got you! So you won't be able to shout your mouth off any more, will you? You'll have to toe the line now, won't you? Or you'll be a BAD PARENT!'

EQUIPMENT

Going down the road to the shops now means packing as much stuff as one used to have for a four-day stay at a mud-logged open-air pop festival. It makes no difference if you drive, walk or cycle, you are still going to have to deal with folding prams, catches, clips, locks, bags and devices which have been brilliantly designed, sure, but which will make you contort your back into insane posi-tions so that baby will be comfy, and which will all, at some point, spring back on your finger or thumb, while the baby cries on. Out of all of these, there's only one I've found that can genuinely be opened and closed with one hand, is easy to get on and off a bus with, and really doesn't weigh very much, and that's the McLaren buggy. We had other pushchairs and prams before which may have provided more support for the baby's back, which may have been able to double, or even treble, as carrycot, pram, Moses basket, car seat, baby feeder, bouncer, and children's entertainer, but the purchase of our McLaren buggy was the first indication of light at the end of the tunnel. Up until then, every minor journey felt like the beginning of an exploratory trek up the Amazon. So much so, one wonders why God didn't make it essential to have three people to create a baby; a mother, a father, and an experienced scaffolding packer.

I recently watched a man reach a state of mind normally only reserved for being on the losing side at a football match, as for half an hour he tried to fit his convertible pram/carrycot into the back of his New Man Fiesta/Fiat, without waking the baby. After ten minutes or so of cut fingers and cursing while he tried it lengthways, sideways, rearranged the sterilised bottles in the boot of the car, took out the nappy bag and put that in the passenger seat, folded down the passenger seat, repositioned the baby car seat, I went up to him and said two words: 'McLaren buggy'.

This is not an advertisement, and this book is not subsidised by McLaren's but the McLaren buggy can change your life. You can hold the baby while you kick the buggy into action with your foot, rather like a motorcycle, and once it starts to slide, it folds all the way to walking-stick size by itself, and snaps shut of its own accord. As you get off the bus, you can flick one catch with your little finger and it just falls open ready to plonk the baby in, needing only a small heel jerk to lock it all in place. No Norman-Wisdom-with-a-deckchair routines with a McLaren buggy. Thank you, McLaren design department, for saving my discs and vertebrae for more pressing tasks, like carrying a sleeping stone and a half's worth of Stanley up thirteen flights of stairs when the lift's broken down.

The amount of equipment on the market is daunting. It's as if you've just taken up a new hobby or sport. You go to the specialist shop, where they'll sell you an entire set of 'what you'll need to start with', except if you'd gone to the shop next door, they would have sold you something entirely different to cater for an entirely different set of problems. When buying our first baby car seat, we were asked by the assistant, 'Do you fly a lot?', an impossible question to answer when you've just had a child. We may never fly again, or spend the rest of our lives on aeroplanes. This child may end up being an airline pilot, for Christ's sake. The reason the shop assistant asked is because there are baby car seats you can lift out of the car and use as a carrycot as you walk on to a plane. If, that is, you have a degree in advanced mechanics, and work out regularly with weights.

There are also changing-tables, with detachable baby bath units. A changing-table is a low, lightweight chest of drawers on wheels which has a padded top with sides to it, so that you can change the baby while standing up and not have to cross the room to reach for a nappy, or a bottle of cream or the baby's clothes. This is all very well if you have room in the nursery in the first place, and are considerably under five foot six or don't mind stooping to thigh level. A changing-table with a built-in bath unit is one where you lift-up the padded top, and underneath is a moulded baby-sized bathtub which you fill from the tap. This little bathtub is gently sloped for really young babies, and is a great idea until it comes to draining the water. There is a little plug, but this just empties on to the chest of drawers below. So you think, 'I'll just lift out the whole bath unit, and carry it sloshing around down the corridor, and pour it down the sink.' More catches and spring clips later, you spill the lot trying to get it through the kitchen door. I blessed the day Stanley was old enough to have a shallow bath in the grown-up bathroom, with, of course, the assistance of another genius invention, the rubber grippy pad you stick on the bottom, to stop him sliding and bumping his head.

There are cots that later turn into beds, beds that can convert to bunks. Before having Stanley around, I thought the sofa bed was the ultimate advance in bedroom technology. A really good piece of plastic to possess is the one which fits into your toilet seat, making it small enough for a little bottom to sit there without falling in and being eaten by the crocodiles. There's nothing wrong with a good old-fashioned potty, of course, it's just that if you can get them used to using the grown-up toilet, you can get them used to flushing it as well – much easier than teaching them to clean out a used potty properly. Even here, though, there is a disturbing range of choice. Not all grown-up toilet seats are the same size, not all kiddy toilet seats clip on the same way. It's more complicated than buying a compatible hi-fi.

There are chair and table sets with wheels to help the child get used to walking, although Stanley only worked out reverse on this, and would hurtle backwards into furniture, windows and people's legs. There are clamp-on sling chairs which you attach to the sides of tables at mealtimes so that the baby can jog up and down and bring the table crashing down on top of him, or, when older, stand up and threaten to practise diving headfirst to the floor. Baby equipment is big business, and unfortunately, like many hobbies and sports, much of this costly gear gets bought and discarded as you work out what's right for you. When the next generation visit their grandparent's attics, cellars or storage cupboards, they will find not old helmets from the war and board games with half the pieces missing, but springless Baby-bouncers, convertible sun-rain hoods for wall-attachment twin sleeping chairs, and an octopus of straps and buckles for slinging the baby on the back, tummy or shoulders of any parent who has mastered parachute-folding drill.

I'm sure all of this would be different with a second

child. Not only would one have learnt that an old magazine jammed into the car window will shield baby from the sun just as well as a stick-on baby-shade gauze, and that baby is just as happy getting clean in the kitchen sink as in his contoured 'Easi-wash' unit (and happier still getting into your bath), but one hopes that having done it once, a lot of the fear will have gone out of it. Being a first-time parent is absolutely terrifying. There is nothing to prepare either of you for the extreme anxiety you will feel. And as with anything you have no idea

first time in the big bath

how to do, it is easy to take advice from anyone who offers it. And this of course includes people who want to sell you things. How are you to know that you'll probably end up changing the baby on the floor anyway? That a colourful squeaky rabbit on wheels will provide less entertainment than a discarded cardboard box from the off-licence?

MORE EQUIPMENT

One piece of high-tech equipment in which we did invest, and which I was pleased to have, was a baby-breathing monitor. It's an incredible invention. Inside a round plastic envelope, two pancake-sized sheets of metal lie on top of each other, wired up to a little box which you put on the shelf. The plates go under the baby's cot mattress and are so sensitive to movement that every time the baby breathes, a little light flashes on in the box above. If the baby stops breathing, the apparatus gives it fifteen seconds or so, and then starts to wail like a fire alarm. I've no idea how fail-safe this device is, but with it we worried less about cot death, and didn't feel we had to sneak into Stanley's bedroom at all times of day and night to check if he was still alive. The disadvantage was that as he learnt to roll over and move about more (and evidently cot death can happen up to eighteen months old), he would roll away from the part of his mattress where the metal plates were, thus setting off the alarm. After a year, the false alarms happened too frequently, and we stopped using it because our nerves could no longer take the middle-of-the-night panicked lunges across the flat to find a very cross baby crying at having been woken again by a wailing siren.

But the fear of cot death was only one of the many new fears that emerged from the lagoon once Stanley was brought home. When he was in his mum's tummy, the fear centred mainly around getting him born safely, for him and for her. After that, I imagined, fear would subside, to be replaced by a sort of confidently responsible feeling. A sort of warm fatherly glow. How naïve can you get?

Apart from the obvious nightmare scenarios the imagination rightfully conjures up of him pulling a saucepan of boiling water on top of himself, finding a knife or razor blade, swallowing a knife or razor blade, electric shocks, falls, car accidents, and major illnesses, there are other wackier fears, which seem to have less grounding in reality: what if I just dropped him now for no reason? What if he got caught in a lift door? What if someone creeps up by the fire escape, breaks in and steals him while I'm in the bathroom? What if the car gets towed away with him in it? What if I lose him in a shop? No everyday activity seemed immune from these subliminal worries, and I had to fight to keep a level head about which fears to listen to, and which to ignore.

The adrenalin that all this excess fear creates can't be good for me. And worrying about what it's doing to me can't be good either. And trying not to worry must be

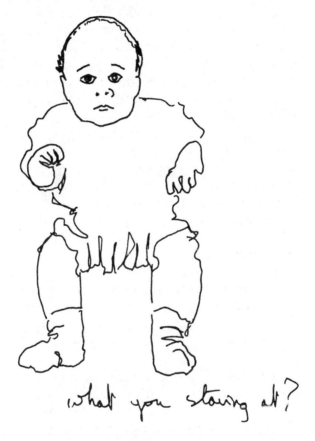

what you staring at?

creating stress. Not having much sleep doesn't help either. And then there are all the cheques I have to write. I have nightmares now about books of cheque stubs, that say things like 'Cot breathing monitor – forty quid', 'Detachable highchair – twenty-five quid', and 'Male bonding self-assertion hypnosis cassettes – two hundred and seventy-five quid' in a voice like Vincent Price. One thing's for sure, once your children have arrived, you can't press 'Pause' ever again, so it's a good idea to have a nice big rest before you start.

TRIVIA

One day, a friend of mine rang to tell me his partner was expecting their first baby. I responded, as one does, with 'How fantastic! Congratulations! How's she feeling? How are you feeling? How's your bank manager feeling?' And he started to drivel on, as one does, about how everything was coming into perspective now, how his whole life now suddenly seemed to make sense. With the grandiose hindsight of one year's experience in this game, I concluded that the poor man was in a state of shock. I recognised the symptoms. At one point he said 'You know, it's great. All the trivial things in life just seem to have gone away!' Not wanting to be the one to burst his bubble by starting a baby-bore conversation with him before he was ready, I merely agreed, and made encouraging noises down the line. 'Ring me and let me know how it went, won't you?' I said, and put down the phone.

Poor bastard. Where does he imagine all those trivial things in life have gone? Into thin air? No, they are multiplying secretly in a bag of amniotic fluid by the second. A baby is a wonderful thing, a miracle, but far from dispersing trivia, it has an unparalleled ability to create trivial things in places where you didn't even know there were places. If you don't keep an eye on the future, you are in danger of becoming forever enmeshed in a dragnet of trivia. Checking food labels for E markings, watching the same *Postman Pat* video everyday for eighteen months, pretending a mouthful of spaghetti is a choo-choo train on its way to Mouth Station, packing, giving away or selling mountains of baby clothes which were grown out of after only three weeks, finding baby-sitters, getting rid of baby-sitters, listening to helpful advice, giving helpful advice, being in for the health visitor, sterilising bottles, plastic bibs, muslin cloths, pushchairs, prams, and converting pounds to kilograms in order to buy the right size of French whole earth disposable nappies.

I'm not saying that these things cannot also be tremendously enjoyable, just that on the Richter Scale of earth-shattering significance, they don't even wake the needle up. These days, I find, men behave over the subjects of childbirth and child-rearing very much as they used to as teenagers in the playground when first discovering girls. 'I took one out last night.' 'Cor, did you? What was it like? Did she let you have a feel?' 'No, but I got as far as number three.' Number three being a kiss with tongues.

There is the same urgent desire to exchange information and show off over something about which they are aware they know pitifully little. Another friend of mine has recently started a fathers' drinking group. Once they've had a few, they get on to the real nitty-gritty stuff about how to stop the baby's sheets getting drenched at night, or useful burping hints.

There is something awe-inspiring about witnessing a child put together the jigsaw pieces of his world. What information he retains as significant, what is left behind, what gets built up into an anxiety. It's a jigsaw that you never want to see completed. This is why people with kids, especially first kids, tend to become rather boring to the outside world, only talk to other people with kids, and don't bother to go out much any more. I used to look at them with pity, but now I know they don't need it. Who needs to go and see a brilliant new movie when you've got a brilliant new person making a mess in your living room? We had some friends over on the night that Stanley first learnt to roll over on to his tummy all by himself. Anna came in screaming from the other room. 'Quick! Come and look! He's turned over!' I dropped everything, stopped being a host, and dashed to see. Yes! He had turned himself over! Amazing! And he was trying to do it again! My God! Quick! A camera! Our friends, not parents themselves, smiled with fixed smiles. and left quite early. We hardly noticed. This funny maggot she had spent so long incubating actually had a will and a spirit of its own. It had practised and achieved a remarkable feat. Put his name down for the Olympic rolling-over team!

When Stanley was about a year old, he started going to a day nursery for one whole day a week. I think this is a much better idea than the old-fashioned nurseries, where you spend all morning getting them there, just have time to come home for a cup of coffee, and then have to go back and pick them up because the nursery stops at lunchtime. I can still remember the first morning at my first nursery. Four years of my mum and brother and then one day, suddenly, plonk, look, here's a boy playing with a train, wouldn't you like to play with him? 'No, of course I wouldn't.' But you'll have a lovely time here. 'You wanna bet? I want to stay with you, and there's no way I'm letting go of you. What is this? After four years, you're suddenly going to shove me in this drafty church hall? You must be joking.' I cried, I clung, I shat myself, anything not to be left there.

These days, when there are so many more mothers who work, there are many more whole-day nurseries around, and they take children at a much earlier age. This is good. The children get a social life, and can be introduced to separation gradually rather than later on in one blinding rent. Mrs Thatcher, of course, would disagree. When she was in power, she tried to discourage this, and was in favour of the old system of nurseries starting at five, and mothers staying with babies until then. But then, she also stopped school milk. Yes, I know, it's rather out of date to knock her now that even she is writing letters all over the place repudiating her own handiwork. But young Stanley was born in 1988, during her third term, and he and I watched her resignation speech together early one morning over a soft-boiled egg and a dippy-dip toast.

SIX

Dear Stanley George Planer,
Can I have my wife back? Just for some of the time? I
know you're the man in her life now, but couldn't we
work out some sort of time-share system? I'd throw in a
cassette recorder as a sales enticement. You could have
her, say, early in the mornings, at mealtimes, and at any
time you're being noisy or messy, and, of course, when
I'm at work, and I could have her the rest of the time . . .
Well, OK, how about four evenings a week, and every
alternate weekend? No? Oh what's the point . . . she's
probably thinking about you when she's with me
anyway. I know I'm thinking about you when I'm with
her. You just carry on as you are, and we'll work round
you. I suddenly feel very old. Also, will you please try to
hold back a bit on being cute and interesting and
adorable? Your mother and I are absolutely shattered
and irritable, and although it's so obviously all your
fault, neither of us has it in us to blame or resent you
one little iota. So we just get angry with each other, or
the broken hoover, or daytime television. Honestly,
can't you try and be a little bit more tactful? Stop being
so funny, just for half a day, why don't you, and let us
be grumpy for a bit. We're trying to have a good old-
fashioned nervous breakdown together, we've worked
for it, we deserve it. So stop cheering us up all the time,
it's rude.

MUMMY

Last year Maeve Haran, a former hotshot TV exec who gave it all up to spend more time with her children, brought out her first novel, *Having It All*, about a hotshot TV exec who gives up being a hotshot TV exec so that she can spend more time with her children. And she was crucified in the press. Not for the quality of the writing, which may or may not have been good, but for daring to suggest that, after a hundred years of woman's struggle, a powerful woman might actually get more job satisfaction out of sitting on the floor with finger paints and watching her children grow than from a power-dressed lunch with the flat-leather-briefcase people. One reviewer even said that the book was in danger of 'glorifying motherhood', which would be a very, very bad thing, of course.

Tests on mothers have proved that they can identify the crying of their own baby, as opposed to the crying of other babies, in their sleep. Fathers, of course, don't have this magic inner radar system. Other tests have shown that when presented with babies – not necessarily their own – women experience dilation of their pupils (an involuntary sign of attraction), whether they already have children or not. In men, however, dilation of the pupils only occurred with those who were already fathers, suggesting that warm parental feelings come naturally to women, but have to be learnt by men.

It took Stanley at least four months to realise that Mummy and he were separate people, and then another six to understand that there was a third concept to take on board: Daddy. Once he'd got that under his belt, he could assimilate grandparents, friends, other people, cats, and Ninja Turtles. There is a natural speed to the acquiring of wisdom, and children are still fitting together the pieces of their internal jigsaw until puberty.

For the first year, it is difficult not to continue to think of Stanley as a thing. He has all the bits that humans have, but he behaves in an almost incomprehensible way. The same could almost be said of his mother. Although the umbilical cord has been cut, and she stops breast-feeding at six months, they seem to be joined together in some way until his first birthday. The pair of them make a sort of single lumpy thing, like a ropy old duvet that has been washed too many times and shoved carelessly into its cover. Human beings have the longest baby- and childhoods of all the mammals, and for the first year Stanley is still totally dependent on his mum. He cannot control his body temperature, cannot sweat or shiver. If he's too cold or too hot, he can only cry.

For the first five months or so, he can't get around by himself at all. He can stick his bottom in the air, or he can push up his shoulders and head, but not both at the same time. This is tremendously frustrating for him, and another cause for crying. And what with hunger every few hours, and boredom at seeing the same episode of *Fluffy Penguin Mobile* again and again, he does tend to

Mother + Child

cry rather a lot. I never realised I needed sleep more than sex, food or money before.

For the first few months it's good for mother and baby to stay very close to each other. A woman uses up fifteen hundred calories a day breast-feeding, so although the baby is no longer tied to her umbilically, they are still really part of the same biological unit. Being separate from each other must take some getting used to, and there's little to be gained by rushing it, which will cause anxiety in them both.

BURPING

Not being a great team sportsman, I've never had a major kiss and cuddle with the boys because one of us scored a goal. Nor have I every caught a batsman out with a brilliant catch and leapt in the air shouting 'Owzat!' while everyone hugs me and pats me on the back. I tried golf once, and despite deriving a certain amount of satisfaction out of the 'tock' noise the ball makes if you hit it hard with your driver, this was soon dissipated when I saw the direction in which the ball had gone.

I do have moments of satisfaction; getting a laugh, bringing something new to a scene in the twentieth take, managing to stop worrying for a whole day, that sort of thing. But nothing really matches up to successfully burping a baby.

When a baby has eaten or drunk, quite often it has swallowed a lot of air. This is evidently because of the horizontal feeding position favoured in the West. The sucking it performs at the mother's nipple is not the casual drinking-straw type we do when sipping a cocktail. It's stronger than the suck you'd give to one of those Polyfilla milk shakes that come with a takeaway hamburger and chips. It's stronger than the suck a manic chainsmoker would give to get a nicotine hit of an eleven-inch cigar. It's coupled with a sort of chomping of the jaw, as the baby mangles your partner's nipple into submission. Afterwards, quite often, they have what we would call indigestion, a gassy pain in their tummy, and until they've burped and sicked this away, they complain in the only way they know how; opening their larynxes and turning the volume up to ten.

There are all sorts of different ways of burping a baby, and each baby seems to have its own favourite method. You can lie him face down on your lap and pat his bottom, you can hold him up to your chest and let him puke up over your shoulder, you can jog him up and down or hold him upside down, and when he's burped enough, he stops crying. But the satisfaction derived is more than just the knowledge that now you might be able to get an hour or so's sleep. The satisfaction, for me anyway, is the feeling that you're part of something, that you are useful, that you have a knack, a special system which works. Being able to bath, dress, bottle-feed, change, clear up poo, fold carrycots, all these things are useful of course, but they don't give the same satisfaction, because in performing them one senses that one is really just an extra pair of hands. Anyone would do, and a mother would undoubtedly do better. I felt very much like an assistant, and a rather annoying one at that.

But burping is different. It's between you and the baby, and requires the same kind of half-absent, half-concentrated attention as a game of darts. It needs timing. When to pat, when to wait. It's an empathy game, and a confidence trick. Watching Anna master her first breast-feeding session with Stanley showed me a little of what might be required. Starting to breast-feed is not always as simple as he cries, you feed him. There's a battle of wills going on. He needs to be shown how to feed without fear. The exact moment to shove a nipple in his mouth has to be sensed, and taken. The mother might panic at the noise the baby's kicking up, or worry about whether she's going to be competent. She has to achieve the right balance between thinking about it, and not thinking about it. Anna and Stanley made a good team within minutes, and he breast-fed for about five and a half months, until one day he decided to move on.

For me, as a man, burping was the nearest I could get

Which end do I put the bottle in?

to some kind of symbiotic relationship with him during the early days. Apart from that, I felt very much on the outside, an observer. Fascinated to note how his focus broadened, how he learnt to grip things, what colours pleased him, what noises he was aware of, but still observing these things from the audience, not actually up on stage with him as she was. As he grows, of course, so does my involvement. The more cognitive he becomes, the greater my function, my usefulness. But in the meantime, I had to make do with the odd bit of wind.

BABY GOES INTO THE OUTSIDE WORLD

Stanley is two months old. His dad has made a film for the BBC, and there's a showing of it in a preview theatre in Soho at eleven o'clock in the morning. I don't feel like going on my own. Anna would like to get out of the house. Let's all go. We'll take Stanley with us. He's being ever so quiet and contented at the moment. He's never been to a cinema. Maybe he'll just fall asleep in the dark. Actually, we both just want to get out there and show him off to everyone.

The proud parents arrive in Soho. The beautiful boy behaves impeccably and charms all the cast and crew at the preview theatre. Until, that is, the moment the lights go down and the opening frames of his dad appear on the screen. Then he starts to cry; unassailable crying. I take him outside so that Anna can see the film. I've seen it before anyway, albeit in the wrong order.

A strange experience, standing in a cold doorway in Soho, rocking new baby, with busy, seedy life bustling past in front of me, and busy, seedy phone calls from the office above the preview theatre wafting out from behind me. An Arthur Daley-type voice is having a profane row about the delivery of some video tapes. In the street opposite a tired-looking woman in a booth is shouting, 'Come in, sir, live show, beautiful girls' at every single male who walks past, whether punk, yuppie, or labourer. A bunch of pissed blokes loiter around outside her establishment, deciding whether to go in or try elsewhere. I've been working, on and off, in the West End for ten years now, but I never really noticed all this before. Well, it never made me feel uncomfortable before. No doubt they all think I'm a plain-clothes policeman, and the baby is just a very clever decoy. By walking him up and down and rocking him a bit, I manage to get his blubbering down to a manageable whimper. After fifteen minutes or so, Anna joins me; she cannot be separated from baby for very long when he is at this age. The film lasts one hour and twelve minutes. A good length for a BBC Screen on 2. A terrible length for standing in a doorway in Soho with a two-month-old baby.

The first time Anna and I went out together for an evening, leaving Stan in the care of a baby-sitter, was no more comfortable an experience than the streets of Soho. We went to the theatre, to which we had been invited by some people who had children over five. Old hands. The first thing our friends said on hearing that this was our baby-sitting debut, was that we were not allowed to leave in the interval, we had to stay to the bitter end. We sat through the first half, nervously holding hands, neither of us having any idea what the play was about, and at the interval, as everyone rushed to the bar to get a drink, we rushed to the call box. We had come prepared, with ten-pence pieces and a phonecard, just in case, to speak to the baby-sitter. No, he hadn't stirred; he was sleeping like a baby. So we had to go back in and see the second half of the meaningless play before being allowed to rush back home, thankful that the cast had only taken three curtain calls. It was a horrible night. Having involved myself a certain amount with Stanley early on, I found it difficult to play what I felt my role should be. That of a confident and reassuring husband to Anna. 'Stop worrying, he'll be fine,' sounded hollow and croaky in my throat as I secretly fantasized our sweet baby-sitter as a baby-snatcher or even baby-axer.

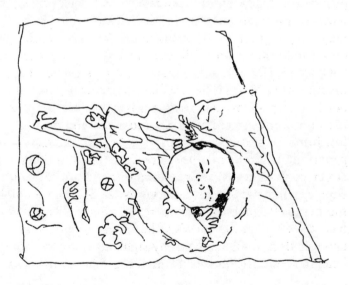

This is a problem for the New Age daddy. It's no good having two scaredy-cat parents wanting to cuddle and nurture. I find myself as soppy as if I had had the baby myself when it comes to letting go of him to a baby-sitter, or to a day nursery. This cannot be what good fathering is about, surely?

FIRST TIME OUT ALONE

A real breakthrough came for me when Anna finished breast-feeding and first trusted me to take Stanley out by myself. This is something that, as a father, really could be my job. Over the course of thirteen years or so, gradually to encourage the child away from dependence. It begins when the baby learns to walk, and walks to Daddy. Away from the warmth of Mummy towards the independent and scary unknown. Depending on the relationship, a first-time dad may meet a certain amount of resistance to this from his partner. He is, after all, taking a part of her away from her.

So there I am, on my first outing, with a tiny sprog in a pushchair. It's a windy Sunday in February, and he's wrapped up warm. The local paper shop is closed, so if I want to get the papers, I'm going to have to walk right down the main road with him, and worse, all the way back again. He's OK now, but what if he starts crying for his mummy? What if he finishes all the soya milk in his bottle and realises that mummy is gone? It'll be ten to fifteen minutes to get back. Should I stop and try to comfort him? Or should I just get back as fast as I can? Will people think that I'm a baby-snatcher as I run down the street pushing a screaming, purple tot, dropping colour supplements and Sunday reviews as we go? Sure enough, moments after buying the papers, Stanley realises that he hasn't seen his mum for all of half an hour, and starts to bawl. If an ambulance went by right now, no one would hear it above the noise he's making. My efforts at the comfort option last about half a minute. No matter how much I would like to be right now, I just am not mummy.

I go for the running method. The poor little sod is clattered up and down on the pavement, people stare as much as if we were leaving a stream of blood behind us, and we get back home with nothing but the business sections of the Sundays intact. Although we've only been gone for three-quarters of an hour, we have to wake Anna from a fairy-story hundred-year sleep. She has been sleeping so deeply she doesn't know where she is or who we are. 'He needs his rest,' she says on automatic, and in about four minutes he is sleeping peacefully. I don't know why I should be surprised when she knows so exactly what he wants, until recently he was, after all, part of her body, but it amazes me every time. That night I dream of when he's old enough to take on camping holidays, or when I might be able to help him with his homework. I certainly don't feel very useful at the present moment.

THE LONE RANGER

When I first took Stanley out in his buggy by myself, I confess I felt embarrassed, self-conscious, and wimpish. This was before I realised what a good deal the New Age dad is getting. Once you've mastered the simple physical difficulty that all baby equipment is made to be used by women, and have found your own way of making it male user friendly, you can definitely have the best of both worlds, image-wise. For instance, if you make the mistake of standing behind the buggy holding both handles, not only will you have to stoop because they are down below your waist, but your feet will kick the back wheels if you take a normal male stride. The thing to do is to stand alongside the buggy, holding only one of the handles, and take as large a stride as you feel you need to preserve your macho image. This enables you not only to do some pretty nifty one-handed kerb-jumping and cor-ner-skidding, but also to be closer to the child for conver-sation and eye contact. Looking good, feeling good.

When you arrive at the playground or park, it's best not to sit around smoking and looking bored on a bench. Either get into that sandpit and play with the child your-self, or read a book or newspaper in a way that says you completely trust the child to be his own person in this environment. If the child falls over and cries, either ignore him, or ignore everyone else and go and kiss and cuddle him ostentatiously. Don't do that self-conscious, panicky half run, half trot towards him, that tells every-one in the playground you're really worried baby might have broken his knee, but you're too embarrassed to show how concerned you are because that might not be manly enough. By the way, for the best results male ego-wise, go to the park or playground without your partner. People may think you're a single parent and pity you, or better still, admire you. Then, as you are about to leave, be sure to say, as loudly as possible, 'Back to mummy now'. This works particularly well early in the morning, because all of the women present will seethe with jeal-ousy, and think you're great. 'Why can't I have a lie-in like that little boy's mum?' they'll be thinking, as you whisk your kid away. All the other fathers, who are trail-ing around with the whole family, will envy the great one-to-one relationship you have with your kid, and wonder why they've come out at all. As you sneak into the sweet shop on the way back to ensure a lasting bond between you and your child, they will no doubt ask, 'Who was that masked man?' 'That was the Lone Ranger.'

The big mistake in all of this is self-consciousness. The Lone Ranger never let on how much of a dickhead he felt in those silly tight white trousers, and nor must you with ice cream down your lapel. Children are pretty intuitive about self-consciousness, and the danger is that a moment of self-doubt from you will be echoed in your child's behaviour.

CONVERSION

Being a parent is like being the agent of a self-centred Hollywood star. Your client says he doesn't like the script because it doesn't make him look sexy enough, or clever enough. You quietly work at convincing him to do the role. You feed his ego. Self-respect, pride and dignity are as important at three as they are at thirty-three. Like any business deal, the best way of winning is showing your opponent a dignified way of giving you exactly what you want. 'I want you to have your bath and go to bed. You need guidance to understand that really that's want you want also.'

One needs terrific self-confidence, almost arrogance, to instil confidence in another. If I have succeeded in finding some of this self-confidence, I don't know where it came from. Before I met Stanley, I was the kind of person who, if I said 'Sit' to a dog, it immediately had a hysterical fit, and if I tried to control a horse, it would throw me. I was useless with children, animals, and people. Relationships were things you got into by mistake, and love was a feeling I had if I really fancied someone a lot. Something happened, and I think it took about four seconds, when they handed me that screaming little blue bundle in the hospital birthing room. In that moment, I understood that love is an action, not a feeling, it's what you consciously decide to do.

Last week I was drinking with some old friends. Two men, my age, who work in recording studios, neither married, neither with children. What are nowadays called 'empty-nesters'. As we left the pub, one of them suggested we cross the road to chat up some girls who were standing on the other side. They knew the girls by sight, and wanted to get to know them more. One of the girls was holding her four-month-old baby boy. After saying, 'What a lovely baby', as one does, my friends began to chat up the single girls. I joined in, but found myself more interested in the baby. The nearest I got to pick-up lines were, 'Does he sleep through the night? Is he having trouble teething? Has he had colic? Oh look, he smiled. Can I smell his scalp?' (Babies scalps. Mmmmm.) All this with an idiotic and beatific grin right across my face.

Whether women find this kind of behaviour in a man more or less attractive than coffee-ad smoothness or macho posing, I have no idea, and I don't care. I've turned from an ignoramus who knew nothing about children and paid them little attention, into an ignoramus who has an idiotic Cheshire-cat smile from ear to ear whenever he sees one, and who is more likely to stare at the contents of a woman's pram than those of her pullover. I'm glad this happened to me when it did, because now I feel I will be ready in time for my midlife crisis.

Any of you girls want a ride in my car?

SEVEN

September 1989

Dear Stanley

*Please hurry up and learn how to look at storybooks.
Your grandma's given you loads of Beatrix Potter
already, and there's monster books, and pirate books,
and even a Jolly Postman book on your shelf, but you
don't really know what they are yet. The only ones you
seem to clock are the pop-up books, which are all very
well but I can't wait to be able to tell you stories and
act out all the voices for you and play.*

*Anna's been checking out the kids' section at the
video shop as well, and there's loads of stuff there. We
saw just about every grown-up video in the shop on all
those evenings when she was pregnant, so I feel ready to
move on to* The Little Mermaid *and* Lady *and the Tramp
and* BFG *now. Come on. You've looked at your mobile
long enough surely. Penguins going round in one
direction, then back again. Stories are much more fun.
Get on with it.*

*Oh, and while you're at it, could you practise crayons
as well, because we've just got new wallpaper in the
corridor, and we don't want you to scribble all over the
place any more. Draw a fish on a piece of paper or
something. OK!*

LEARNING TO TALK

When Stanley was about ten months old, he started to develop a rash all over his back and on his legs. We took him to a doctor, who recommended a skin specialist. Having suffered from eczema when I was a child, I was wary of what the doctors might do. I had had all kinds of cortisone creams, which although they temporarily removed the rash, had no long-term benefits. I have loathsome memories of going on dairy-exclusion diets to clean up my skin.

The skin specialist was not at all what I was expecting, and very different from all the ones I had been to as a child. She was a charismatic Eastern European woman, more the type to whom you could imagine confessing your dreams and fantasies while stretched out on a couch for fifty guineas a throw, than one of those white-coated dermatologists with a pen in one hand and a prescription pad in the other that I had grown used to. The first thing she did, after looking at his back, was to talk to Stanley.

'What a clever boy you are,' she said. 'You can't talk yet, but you've found a way to express yourself, haven't you?' He gurgled and wriggled on Anna's lap. The woman looked up at us and said, 'This is his little rebellion. He can't tell you what is wrong yet, so he's showing you. What's it like at home? Is there some stress there which you are keeping from him?'

Was there some stress? Was she a comedian as well? Well, apart from the devils in our washing machine, which I've already talked about, and apart from neither of us having had any sleep for months, yes, we did have the slight problem of builders. Every room in the flat was being done. Walls were coming down, walls were going up. We were trying to rearrange the tip I had lived in before I met Anna into a suitable home for three, and because we were living there at the same time, there wasn't a day when all of the furniture did not have to be moved from one room to another. Plumbers and carpenters had keys and would come and go at strange hours, or not turn up for a few days on end, as is their habit. Through all this Anna had struggled brilliantly to keep Stanley's meal-, bed- and bathtimes regular, and we had agreed that the one room which should not be turned upside down was his. In fact, concerned that all this upheaval would disturb him, we had given ourselves extra stress by making sure that we kept him away from the worst of it to protect him. Wrong.

'Why don't you tell him what's going on?' the woman said, in a voice straight out of a Woody Allen movie. 'Talk to him, use long words if you like. Talk to him as an equal, then he can stop worrying about it. He may not understand exactly what you're saying, but he will get the meaning all right. At the moment you're leaving it all to his imagination, and goodness knows what terrifying conclusions he is reaching from your unwillingness to let him in.' Breakthrough.

There is an old stand-up comedian's joke which goes, 'Until I was sixteen, I thought my name was shut up', and when you suddenly have a noisy, messy demanding thing which has just learnt to crawl, bombing around your home, trying to put its fingers into plug sockets, tear plants apart, and pull heavy furniture down onto itself, it is hard indeed to do anything but run around after it saying 'No', turning yourself, in the process, into an exhausted, self-hating zombie. It is easy at this stage to become disappointed in yourself for thinking of the child as some stranger from another planet. You wanted something to care for. What you got was yet another person who does things their own way, and who has to be understood and negotiated with. Getting an unwilling toddler's socks and shoes on in the morning makes American plea bargaining look sissy. If, however, you give the child the benefit of the doubt for a minute, and assume that whatever he does, however annoying or stupid it might seem, he has a good reason for doing it, things become less, not more, tiring.

For instance, baby spends the first four months at least coming to the humiliating realisation that it is not God. Up until then, when it was hungry, the world was hungry; when it moved its arms and legs, the world moved its arms and legs. Not understanding this from the child's point of view will lead to less sleep in the end. The realisation that it cannot always control mother, and that she does not necessarily come the moment it is hungry, that she is, in fact, separate, makes it pretty angry. 'You mean there are people around who I don't have completely under my control?'

In trying to protect Stanley from the stress of the builders, and keep what we were going through from him, we had been patronising him, treating him like an alien. As if we had thought of him as a lump of clay, which it was up to us to mould, and for which we would be solely responsible.

Stanley was introduced to the builders, and told what they were up to. 'This is Mr Neville, and he's sawing up wood so that we can have a cupboard to put our clothes in instead of having them slung all over the sofa, and this is Peter, he's painting the walls, that's why we can't go in there just yet, and this is where the plumber should have joined up the hot-water pipes but we haven't seen him for weeks and that's way we have to boil the water for your bath.' He listened with rapt attention. He began to look forward to the arrival of the builders, he learnt their names, he stole their tools, he got in their way. He named some of his toys after the builders, and for a while would not go anywhere without a little plastic troll he called 'Peter'. When he had learned to walk (the builders were there for a very long time), he used to hang around them with his own plastic hammer and paintbrush, and try to help with their work. The rash became irrelevant and eventually disappeared.

LEARNING TO LISTEN

Having discovered that there were things other than 'No' which we could say to Stanley was immensely helpful. Discipline is a funny thing. Mere insistence that, as a parent, your view of a given situation is to prevail, and your rules are to be obeyed, does not guarantee that the child accepts any of it in his heart, even if he does exactly what you ask. Working to rule, and the accompanying harboured resentments, start at the year dot. If I cannot, or do not, know how to listen to my child, how can I expect him to listen to me or my commands?

In the long run, I seem to have an easier life all round when I manage to interpret what it is he is trying to tell me. I know from my own schooldays that there is an immense difference in how it feels to obey a command, and how it feels to control myself and make my own decisions. So, the trick is to make him feel as though he thought of it himself. Egotistical little bugger. Takes after his father, no doubt. Learning to read your child's behaviour, that's the knack to acquire. Some of it is pretty bizarre and can be extremely irritating as well as unbearably cute. So when he's lying on his back thrashing his arms and legs around like a helicopter, he might be thinking. 'How many years' practice does it take just to roll over'? And when he throws his teddy, or dummy, out of the cot onto the floor, and you pick it up only to have him throw it out again, and again, he might not be thinking, 'Great, Dad's nearly at the end of his tether, let's see how far I can push him', but 'How much of this environment is under my control?' The repetition could be just like a scientific experiment or a poll. 'Is there a pattern to this? Do dummies disappear every fourth throw, or do they always come back?' The child is working hard all the time.

The 'terrible twos' are proverbially when children start to have really big temper tantrums. And in our case, we found the expression to be right. But it's not much help knowing that this is perfectly normal behaviour for that age when you're trying to handle a thrashing octopus which makes as much noise as a car alarm, and is as likely to go off without any warning or provocation. However, if you think about it, for the child the first two years must be like trying to find your way into the most sensationally complicated computer program, and if after two years' practice, you press what you thought was the right key, and something completely different from what you expected flashes up on the screen, taking you right back to lesson one, you would have a temper tantrum too. Well, I would. But then I find setting the video a major test of patience.

For instance, out shopping with Stan, I have an easier time if I say, 'How many red things can you see in this shop?' than if I say 'Don't touch anything, keep the noise down and keep still', and if, instead of simply correcting mistakes, I take an interest in how they were made. For a child to say 'mouses' instead of 'mice' is incorrect, but it's still a pretty brilliant mistake to have made, because it means he has heard the word mouse at one time, and heard people putting an 's' on things when there are more than one of them at other times, and he has then made an incredible imaginative leap and put the two concepts together. 'Mouses'. Stunning.

A towny friend of mine took his son out to the country for the first time, and they drove past some sheep, which the boy had never seen before. Without hesitating, the child said 'Oh look Daddy, cloud-dogs.' That is not just cute, it's genius.

MAGIC AND FANTASY

Growing up seems to happen in fits and starts. Weeks of food-splattering and drink-spilling will go by, and then suddenly he does it all in one huge leap, overnight. You can wake up in the morning and notice a new look behind his eyes, and feel a stranger to him.

Suddenly, after being at the 'I want a drink' stage for as long as you can remember, he has twenty or thirty new

join me for breakfast?

words in his vocabulary, and can construct complex sentences like 'Let me choose which egg I want', and 'But I don't want to have my bath because I cleaned my face with a tissue already.'

His memory is also extraordinary in its selectivity. Details that seem trivial to us are stored and reiterated sometimes up to a year later. He remembers that he got a balloon in a shop you haven't been to for eight months. When he was two, Stan remembered the way to a friend of mine's house, and cried when I missed the turning. I couldn't understand why the tears, and was amazed when he said, 'Daddy lost, Daddy miss it'. I hadn't realised that he was aware of the streets going by, let alone that he was ready to take the London taxi drivers' 'knowledge' exams.

On our kitchen wall is a large poster of Laurel and Hardy. At first, Stan is worried by these two large black-

and-white faces peering over his shoulder every time he eats his supper, so I talk to him about them. 'The one scratching his head is called Stanley, just like you.' He points at Oliver Hardy, and says 'Daddy'. Thank you, Stan. I'm the big fat exasperated one, am I? But at least he has his first appreciation of a comedy double act. He calls them Stanley and Daddy. We get out an old Laurel and Hardy video and Stan finds it hilarious. Ladies slipping on custard pies, custard pies in people's faces, and a lot of shin-kicking. The shin-kicking delights him particularly, and he tries it out on me, and everyone who comes to the flat. We have to try and teach him the difference between fiction and reality. It's OK for Stanely and Daddy to do it on the video, but not OK for him to do it in the living room. This is a shame, because at his age there is no difference between fantasy and reality; they complement each other. Fantasy helps make sense of reality, and vice versa. If he complains of a scary monster in his bedroom, it is a real monster, and he has to be given the equipment to get rid of it, such as laughing at it, playing monsters, or telling it to go away. It will not help him to say there's no such thing. He would know you were lying, because that monster really is scaring him.

'Many parents believe that only conscious reality, or pleasant and wish-fulfilling images should be presented to the child – that he should be exposed only to the sunny side of things . . . '(Bruno Bettelheim, *The Uses of Enchantment*). Protecting him from scary monsters, or denying their existence, would not only give him a false sense of reality, it would also make redundant his fantasy life. Shortly after our new wallpaper is up in the corridor, Stanley whispers mysteriously to me to follow him. He leads me secretly to a dark corner of the corridor, behind the bathroom door. He points to an area about six inches square where there are wax crayon scribbles all over the new wallpaper. 'Ssshhh', he whispers, 'Naughty.' 'Yes,' I say, 'definitely very naughty, I wonder who did that?' 'Uncle Russell did it,' he replies. Not Uncle Russell again. Most children are supposed to invent a fictional character who they can blame for all their own naughtiness. Stanley, for some reason, has chosen his Uncle Russell. I probably wouldn't have noticed the scribbles down there for months, if not years, and I haven't got it in me to dismiss the Uncle Russell fantasy and give Stanley a telling-off. So I go along with it, and make out that I believe his uncle would have come round secretly and scribbled on the hall wall with wax crayons. No doubt this is taking it too far and when he's a teenager I will pay for it.

Knowing exactly when to indulge fantasy and when to bring in harsh reality is really difficult. Obviously, crossing a road for example, needs an uncompromising dose of the latter; reading a story, the former. But there are vast grey areas where the two cross over, and where one doesn't want to curb a child's imagination. Not just because the imagination is such a lyrical, wonderful, airy-fairy thing, but because it is such an important learning device.

I take Stan for a walk one morning, and we pass a parked red Royal Mail van. 'Look, Postman Pat, Postman Pat,' he shouts. 'Yes, well it is like Postman Pat, it's a mail van, yes, but . . .' 'Where's Jess?' he asks. I lift him up to look in at the window. There's no black-and-white cat on the passenger seat. 'Jess must have gone for his dinner,' I say. Then I spot the postman coming back from the letter box. Unfortunately, this postman does not look one eency-weency bit like Postman Pat. He is wearing jeans and trainers, is smoking a roll-up, and worst of all, he has no hat! He does not look as if he has the time to play with a two-year-old boy either. He looks as though if we were to ask him were his hat is, or where his black-and-white cat is, he would tell us to fuck off. I chicken out and whisk Stanley away. 'Well, Postman Pat must be having a cup of tea with Mrs Goggins right now.' I distract him so that he doesn't look back over his shoulder and see the harsh reality that not only does our postman not have a hat or a blue uniform, he does not even say, 'Cheerio'.

Now he is nearly three, Stanley has a curved piece of railway track which he calls his gun, and which he fires at people, making a 'Keeyoo, keeyoo', noise. Sometimes this noise sounds more like 'Kill, kill', a word he must have picked up from somewhere while we were out doing our best to make the world a better place for folks to live in. This morning, while I was trying to write this chapter, he shot me a few times, and then got bored, so he thought he'd go to the other room, where Anna was having breakfast, and try shooting her.

'Daddy?' he said.

'Yes?'

'I'm just going to go and kill Mummy . . .'

I tried to explain to him that he was nearly old enough to be going through his Oedipal stage, and that really he

no fires today

should harbour the desire to kill *me*, and sleep with her, and that it was my job to allow those dark fantasies space, while at the same time retaining a firm but kind discipline, but then I had to get on with the book, so I just said, 'OK,' and left him to it.

'The knowledge of how to build a nest in a bare tree, how to fly to the wintering place, how to perform the mating dance – all of this information is stored in the reservoirs of a bird's instinctual brain. But human beings, sensing how much flexibility they might need in meeting new situations, decided to store this sort of knowledge out-side the instinctual system; they stored it in stories.' (Robert Bly, *Iron John*.)

In the nursery late at night, an aggressive or unpleas-ant feeling can easily be turned into a monster or a creepy-crawly; 'I don't like being frightened by my own nasty feelings, it's easier being frightened by a horrible scary bogey-person'. This is why children like being told scary stories by their parents. If, with the use of fairy stores, you can go through with them the experience of being scared of the monsters, and show them that that's OK as far as you're concerned, you are helping them to overcome their inner fears, and showing them that their nasty feelings are survivable, and most importantly, acceptable to you. This enables them to draw a more use-ful map of the world in which they can cope with their own aggressions and anxieties. We go on needing scary monsters and fairy stories for the rest of our lives: *Termi-nator, Robocop, Jaws*.

The first time I try to make up a story for Stanley instead of reading from a book is a salutary experience, requiring as much concentration and nerve as doing a show. He is late for bed and so has agreed to go without his usual storybook ceremony. 'I'll tell you one instead,' I offer, thinking this will be a quicker and easier way to get him to sleep than *Oscar Got the Blame* or *Sidney the Seven Dinners Cat*. And in I dive, innocent of what I have let myself in for, and with not the slightest idea what the story will be about.

In a second, Stanley's expression becomes transfixed. His eyes widen and he becomes quiet. He looks at me with total concentration and trust. Oh dear. 'Well . . . erm . . . there was a little boy . . . who . . . erm . . . went to a playground one day, and . . .'. This had better be good, because he seems to have total confidence in me and I can't let him down. 'And he met a naughty little girl . . . and she was called . . . erm . . . What was she called?' Without blinking, he replies, 'Cojiflop.' Phew! 'That's right, she was called Cojiflop, and . . .' I continue for a few minutes, stringing arbitrary events together, all the time searching in my mind for an adequate finish. A conclusion that will make the adventures of Cojiflop and the little boy have some point, and, more importantly, a satisfying, sleep-inducing effect. After swinging too high on the swings in the playground, they fly into the sky and hitch a ride in Santa's sleigh back home, where Cojiflop throws the contents of the fridge on to the floor. Naughty Cojiflop. When I'm finished, Stanley asks me to tell it again, as if it was more than a load of rubbish that slipped into my head. I tell him it again, and he agrees to go to sleep. As he's nodding off, he says, 'That little boy was me, wasn't he?' 'Yes of course,' I say, and leave the room humbled. I'll have to think of something better than that next time.

EIGHT

Dear Stan,

It's an awful world to bring you into, I know. We humans seem to have got it wrong, and you may be the last, or last but one, generation of us. Sorry about that. But I just had to do it. I would have missed you terribly otherwise. Just because we seem to be a bunch of dinosaurs, there's no need to give up on it completely, I suppose. The brontosaurus would have looked pretty silly if it had said, 'I suspect we're going to be extinct pretty soon anyway, so I think I'll just give up breeding now to speed the process along.' Anyhow, maybe you will be the one to sort out all of the world's environmental, political and spiritual problems once and for all. Maybe you will be the one with THE ANSWER. That would be nice, to be dad to the new Messiah. Stan of Hammersmith.

BRIGHTER CHILD

Ducks are said to assume that the first thing they clap eyes on when they get out of their shells is their mum. I saw a nature documentary on TV in which a man had a gaggle of Canada geese who had bonded in this way to his Land Rover, enabling him to make extraordinary films of them in flight. Humans are slightly different, although in the case of the male of the species, bonding with a car is not as unusual as it is in geese. But whether bonding to a mother, a Land Rover or a blanket, humans all take a bit longer than ducks or geese. Humans spend the first nine months or so of their lives forming an attachment that they then seem to spend the rest of their lives worrying about losing. The balance between the fear of abandonment and the need for security is the see-saw we are all on, and the method by which we work out who we are.

It's interesting that autistic children are apparently unaware of their own existence. Autism has sometimes been defined as a condition where 'I' is missing from the vocabulary. An autistic child has not realised that the world is not him. Among suggested 'cures' for autism is a system where the mother holds the child and tries to force it to make eye contact, often shouting repeated demands at it, as if the realisation that there is someone else there is what is missing. It is illuminating to think that the way in which the concept of oneself is first developed is through contact with another. How could you realise you exist, if you didn't realise that there is something out there like you, but not you?

In the first three months, eye contact with the mother is probably as important as physical contact and nourishment. Each time the baby smiles back or reacts to stimuli, it is passing another exam in the baby GCSE course on the nature of existence. It can learn by imitation. If it pulls a face or makes a sound and you (or more importantly, the mother), pull the same face back, or make the same noise, it has had its first lesson in geography. If it recognises what you're doing and responds by imitating you in return, or by smiling at how stupid you look, it deserves a gold star. It sounds soppy, but it's a miracle to watch a mother with a young baby involved in this natural give-and-take. She may look as if she's just gone gaga over the new arrival, but actually they are both still working hard at bringing the child into the world. As a dad you can do a bit of this, I suppose, but it's not the same, and you're probably better off fixing the mobile above the cot, doing the ironing, and keeping your partner's other commitments to a minimum. Not that I did any of these. No. I just sat around gazing at them both, going 'Aaah', and making a mess in the rest of the flat.

Once the duckling or cygnet has decided who it's mother is, be it Land Rover or otherwise, this imprint cannot be erased or re-learnt. The period for assimilating this knowledge is shortly after shell-shattering time, and only then. In the same way, human babies have stages of development in which they are most sensitive to certain types of learning. For instance, between six and twelve months is the best time to learn mobility, grasping, crawling, and then walking. Between one and three years, language; between four and six, increased vocabulary. Evidently, a second language will never be so easy to pick up as it is between the ages of four and six, especially if one sets aside a specific, regular time of the week in which it is spoken. We tend to forget that as well as the body, the brain and its capacity are growing at an unprecedented rate for the first five or six years. Half the brain's eventual capacity has been reached by the age of four, and 80 per cent of it by eight.

The implications of this are enough to make me turn to drink. You mean, if we don't provide a stimulating enough environment, our child will be permanently in love with a Land Rover? If he misses one of these vital stages because we went to the cinema that night, he'll never be able to do his sums? You mean we can't just shove a dummy in his gob, stick him in a playpen, and watch *Blockbusters?* At what brain capacity did I get stuck? Didn't my parents realise that I could have been multilingual by the age of three, and now it's too late, and I'll never be able to order a coffee in Walloon?

Between the ages of one and three is when the child really gets the measure of the world into which it has arrived. In this period, patterns and routines are really helpful. Repetition is the tool the child uses to test out the nature of the world it finds itself in. 'When you've had your supper, then you have a bath. Then you go to bed.'

TELEVISION

You know those annoying tunes you hate, usually from an advertising jingle or pop song, which you just cannot get out of your head for days on end? Then you hear someone else humming it absent-mindedly, and smile sympathetically, 'You too, eh?' Nothing you can do, no record you put on, no other tune you whistle, will eliminate this bit of trivia from the shallows of your consciousness, until, like a victim of tap-dripping torture, you admit defeat, and learn to live with the melody in your sleeping and waking hours. These are the kind of tunes that composers, naturally, crave to write, since they too have to earn a living, but I sometimes wish they would restrain themselves a bit, and take our nerves into consideration.

Sometimes, a peculiar line of dialogue from a film or TV programme will have a similar effect on me. I had to live with a line from Cimino's *Heaven's Gate* for several months. The bit where Kris Kristofferson turns to Christopher Walken and says, with gravity, 'You begin to sound like a man with a paper arsehole, Jim', would pop into my mind when I least wanted it – on stage, on a film set, when trying to make polite conversation, at job interviews, while drifting off to sleep. Whenever there was a minor hiatus in the flow of my conscious thought, 'You begin to sound like a man with a paper arsehole, Jim' would jump in and fill the gap. Probably because it's such an incongruous and bizarre thing to say, even in a Michael Cimino movie.

For the last year and a half I have been suffering from an inability to escape from a line Granny Dryden says to Postman Pat in the *'Pat's Windy Day'* episode from the Postman Pat video collection, volume three. The scene is this: it's a windy day, and Pat's hat has blown off and fallen into a stream. He has decided to carry on posting letters without it. He has been to Thompson Ground and Ted Glen's, and finally he arrives at Granny Dryden's. She remarks that he hasn't got his hat on; he tells her it has blown off in the wind; she says, in her puppet's falsetto, that earlier on she saw a postman's hat on the scarecrow, but she 'didn't see how it could be yours'. The first time I heard this, I didn't really notice it. It was only after months and months of repeated viewings with Stanley at breakfast time, that this line really started to get to me. Pat is the only postman in Greendale, right? And every day he turns up wearing his hat, right? Granny Dryden saw a hat looking just like Pat's on a scarecrow on a windy day, and then, next thing, Pat turns up without his hat on for the first time ever. And yet . . . and yet, Granny Dryden still says: 'I didn't see how it could be yours.'

What are we meant to think? That Granny Dryden, despite managing to knit endlessly, cook, and hold otherwise decent conversations, is monumentally, catastrophically stupid? Or is she just winding Pat up? Or are they sharing some private secret? Is she afraid of what the neighbours will think if she is seen to be intimate about Pat's attire? Is she in fact covering up a years' old crush on Pat? Were they indeed lovers once? What is the meaning behind her seemingly offhand remark, 'I didn't see how it could be yours'? Why couldn't she see? It's obviously his hat. Should she be certified? Of course she isn't, and they retrieve Pat's hat and all is well, except that 'I didn't see how it could be yours' is now superglued to the inside of my skull. When telephoning people at work: 'Hello, I looked up your number in my phone book, then dialled it, and you picked up the phone, but I didn't see how it could be yours.' When picking up the coats to go home after a party: 'I bought you this coat for your birthday, do you remember? But when I went to pick it up just now, I didn't see how it could be yours.' When making the coffee: 'I know you like white with no sugar, and this one is white no sugar, but I didn't see how it could be yours.'

The best way of dealing with these annoying tape loops of the brain is to turn them into mantras. Use them to hypnotise yourself. Like people who live near the airport saying, 'Oh, you don't notice the planes after a while.' Zen priests are said to spend years of their lives staring at a blank white wall; if their minds wander for a second, they are beaten by the Zen master. I seem to have spent years of my life now watching 'Pat's Windy Day', and I'm sure that if I could adopt a Zen approach to this, I would reap spiritual benefits. As I reach enlightenment, I would be able to write books such as *The Inner Postman Pat*, and *Zen and the Art of Posting Letters if You're a Puppet*. Children, with their radiant and innocent intelligence, seem to know the value of repetition more than we, with our rat-race mentalities, do. The trick is not to think 'What else, more useful, could I be doing?', but "Pat's Windy Day' must have been sent to me as an exercise, a test of my spiritual development'. Solving why Granny Dryden didn't see that the hat on the scarecrow could be one and the same as Pat's hat, is a Zen riddle on a par with 'What is the sound of one hand clapping?' One would never consciously be able to express the answer even if one found it, so one eats one's

114

breakfast, one gets on with one's day, and all is well. I think I'm going to miss it when Stanley graduates to Turtles or Mickey Mouse.

Stanley not only learnt how to say 'video', but also how to operate it around the time he learnt to say 'Mummy' and 'Daddy', if not slightly before. This might be because the video recorder is kept so near to the floor, but more likely it has to do with his early fascination for anything with knobs and switches on it. The first number he learnt was eight, the channel to which our video machine is tuned. He can't yet set the timer, but then who can?

We are all meant to know that too much television is bad for young children. It is said to make them passive, to dull their curiosity and turn them into couch potatoes, just like their parents. However, to ration it strictly might make it into something extremely desirable and special. Controlling what your children see and don't see on telly is a very difficult and subtle business. When you've had very little sleep, and are very tired of running around clearing up toys and mess, and you know that to shove the child in front of the telly for an hour or so would give you some peace, the last thing you want is a horrid little voice picking away at your conscience, saying: 'Don't you know TV is bad for kids? What kind of a parent are you?' The horrible truth is that anything that goes on too long without attention and stimulation from you is bad for your child. The American 'How to Make Your Child into a Genius' brigade would claim that it's not TV as such that is bad for your kids, but your absence. TV is very good for your children if you sit and watch it with them, and talk to them about what they're seeing. 'What's that woman doing?' 'What colour is that man's hat?' In this respect, the trouble with TV, as opposed to books, or toys, or games, is that it presents great masses of information for which children don't have enough background knowledge. They can't separate

115

make-believe from reality, and this overload of information is what dulls their senses.

This is why I thank God for videos. A story which they can see again and again is much better than a meandering magazine show with countless different items broken up by advertisements. Stanley has his own collection of favourite videos, and some mornings nowadays he doesn't bother to wake us up, but will go and watch a few before breakfast. This gives us an extra hour's sleep or so, and having a properly rested mum and dad is better for him than any 'How to Stimulate Your Child' theory. It does mean, unfortunately, that he has become obsessed with letters and post vans, and we often get called Mrs Goggins or Granny Dryden instead of Mummy and Daddy. But the advantages are numerous.

ONLY CHILD

Some smug bastards would say that I'm totally unqualified to write about parenting, only having the one child. And probably they're right. Some people say it's easier with two, others that it's twice as hard. Some that four is 'one too many', others that you shouldn't stop until you have at least thirty grandchildren, no matter how expensive this makes Christmastime. But very rarely does anyone say that it's OK to stop at one. It's better for a child to have a brother or sister, you might as well get it all done at once, you can't really call yourself a family until there's more than one, etc., etc. Everyone seems to have their own idea, also, about what is the correct age gap, but they generally agree that a year is too little, and five years or over, too much. Even Stanley thinks that an only child is disadvantaged, although were he to understand what having another would actually entail, he might be less sure.

Recently, when I picked him up from nursery, and asked him what he'd been doing all day, he told me he had been playing with Francesco, and Jules, and Jules' baby sister. Then he said, with confidence, 'I need a baby sister. Do you need one, Daddy?' I said it would be quite nice, yes. 'Mummy's going to get one from the shop. A small one. I can carry it in my bag.' I told him in a general sort of a way about the miracle of conception and how long it would take his mum to get one, that it might be a baby brother not a baby sister, and that when it was thirsty it would have to take a drink from Mummy's bosom. He didn't seem to mind that idea too much, because, he explained, he could have some Ribena with a big straw. What he wanted to know was why. Why would it get thirsty, why would it take a long time, why did he need one in the first place? At the moment, he asks why more often than blinking. Not just about things he's seen, but about himself as well. 'Daddy, I want a drink.'

'OK, I'll get you one.'

'Why do I want a drink, Daddy?'

'Because you're thirsty.'

'Why am I thirsty?'

'Because you haven't had a drink for a while.'

'Why haven't I had a drink for a while?'

'Because you weren't thirsty.'

'Why wasn't I thirsty?'

And on and on and on. In the end, having steered clear of 'Because I say so', and 'Because God made it like that', I usually give up, saying, 'I don't know.' I'm sure that's not what you're supposed to do. There is probably a psychologist somewhere who could explain how much damage I've done to my child, and if I ever find that psychologist, I'm going to ask them why until they have to be certified.

John Cleese and Neil Kinnock are only children. I'm not. I can't imagine what it must feel like not to have siblings with whom to compare yourself. The more children you have, the less exclusive attention you can give to each individual. Whether this is detrimental to the child or not depends, I suppose, on the quality of your exclusive attention.

Some people would like their children to be geniuses, whether they have one or more, and put the pressure on from an early age. God knows why. Perhaps so that they can bask in the reflected glory they imagine this would bestow. These vanity-extension children have a rough time, especially at school, where they can become anxious because they fear that their achievements are more important to their parents than they themselves are. It's one thing to take a supportive and encouraging interest in your child's abilities and qualifications, but another to make the giving of love seem conditional on sporting or academic successes, or other skills.

Einstein could not speak at all until he was over three. Until then he communicated through jigsaws and puzzles. An inability in one direction might reveal an enormous ability somewhere else. Danny Kaye, the great American comedian, was also a master chef and a conductor, but he was said to be a rather miserable, grumpy sod when not cooking, conducting or comedying. To respect genius in itself is rather pointless. Genius just means extra power. To say a man or woman is a genius is merely to say they are 'well-endowed', like being large-breasted or hung like a horse. Of course, I'm just jealous, because I don't tend to get called a genius, anymore than I get complimented on the size of my breasts, or the equine proportions of my private parts.

It would seem that genius is not genetic but is brought about circumstantially, particularly in the first five years of life, either by training or by trauma. Mozart, for instance, was coached from the year dot by his obsessive father. Picasso witnessed a massive earthquake when he was three in the same week as witnessing the birth of his sister. The special endowment comes about through a coincidence of circumstances. Geniuses are people who by change find themselves with the most appropriate background to allow them to become a conduit for the desires of their age. Hitler didn't think up Fascism all by himself, he was in the right place, with the right personality disorder, at the right time. It's what one makes of the small or large endowment one has that is significant. Size doesn't matter. It really doesn't. Well, at least that's what people with small breasts and penises say. (Or so I'm told.)

Getting hooked on your child's achievements is easily done, though. When Stanley remembers his numbers, or a complicated new word, both of us go all trembly. When people say, 'Oh he's very clever, is he really only two?', naturally we swell with pride. When we see him not managing to do something through being too timid, too foolhardy, or just plain stupid, it's like lead in our stomachs. It's hard to keep reminding ourselves that children are just 'ordinary miracles', that despite so much of what makes them who they are being down to us, in the end they will succeed or fail despite us, not because of us. Bringing them up is a delicate business. Neither all hands-on, nor all hands-off. I suppose it's rather like cooking, or conducting, or comedy.

THE BEST AGE

I am sitting in the location catering bus for a TV series. As usual, filming is slow, and there's a lot of time for loafing about and talking. An actor, a lighting rigger and a continuity person are talking children. Now that I have one, I am included in the inner circle. 'How old?' 'Nearly two.' 'Aaah, the best age.' People have been saying that since he was born.

These location parents are discussing the subject of bullying at school, and what to do about it as a parent. The actor's nine-year-old son is being bullied, and family life is becoming hell. As a dad, he doesn't know whether to talk to the teacher, talk to the parents of the aggressors, talk to the aggressors themselves and give them a fright, tell his own child to turn the other cheek, or to stick up for himself and fight nasty. Advice is forthcoming from the continuity person. Speak to the teacher first, and find out more about the parents of the aggressors, then, if still necessary, speak to them. Advice of a different nature is forthcoming from the lighting rigger. 'I know this is wrong, but it's the way I was brought up, and it's what I tell my boys,' he says. 'Wait until the bastards' backs are turned, then pick up a brick and make sure they never walk again.' I must remember to tell Stanley never to bully this guy's boys, not that he would, surely? He's all sweetness and light. Maybe nearly two is the best age.

Until seeing these three concerned faces, who have obviously been through a lot more than I have in the wild and wacky world of parenting, I must have been living in dreamtime. I thought parenting was about going 'Aaah!' at tiny pairs of lace-up boots, finding furniture with his name painted on it fantastically exciting, discovering that his fingernails are as soft as paper when you trim them with those blunted-off scissors, music boxes and mobiles, fontanelles, and fish fingers.

Should I be toughening up my attitude? Should I be playing 'See if you can prevent me from walking' games, instead of teaching him animal noises that make me laugh? Naaa. If this is the best age, then we might as well enjoy it. It's more fun asking him to name all the parts of his body or count how many red cars he can see on a journey, or getting him to make animal noises. He has quite a repertoire now. Monkey: oo oo oo; elephant: woooo; dog: woof woof; cat: miaow purr; tiger: grrr; etc. All with accompanying physical impression. And one particularly good thing is that now he can get out of his cot by himself, he sometimes potters about the flat or plays with his toys before waking us up, which means we can get an extra half an hour or so of sleep. The morning after the filming – which went on late into the night – is one of those days, and I roll over and stretch, half awake. 'Ah. It's so good to get a lie-in.' ROAR. From under the bedclothes comes a pouncing two-year old king of the jungle baring its claws. 'No, Stan, lie-in, not lion.' ROAR. Definitely the best age.

NINE

Autumn 1991

Dear Stan,

I don't know if you remember a morning in 1990, probably not, considering you were just two at the time, but since you are now going to be a father yourself, read on. This is what it was like.

Five-thirty a.m.! 'Daddy, Daddeee! Daddeeeeee!' Woken up by crying, screaming, coughing, trying to make himself sick . . . It's her turn . . . It must be her turn . . . It is her turn. Why isn't she even rolling over? She must be faking so that she can lie in through this racket. She's not moving a muscle. It's her bloody turn. There's dramatic wailing and spluttering now from next door. How can he do such an effective impression of the last scene of Jaws without having seen the film? A genetic memory? I can't sleep now anyway, so it might as well be me even though it is her turn . . . And she'll be really grateful, and I'll look really brilliant, if I manage to calm him down and make it all right, and he is calling 'Daddeeeeee', not Mummy. Bugger it. I'm awake now. I might as well get up anyway. Yes, I'm getting up. Pretty virtuous. Yes, and I was in bed an hour and a quarter later than her last night as well . . . which means that if she gets up at nine, she will have had, let me see now, four and three-quarter hours more sleep than me. I might be able to reclaim that next week. Ow! My toe! Did somebody move the bed? It's still dark. I know, maybe if I just show him that it's still dark, and tell him everyone's asleep, and cuddle him a

bit, he'll understand fully, and go back to sleep
completely reassured.

'No. Possman Pat bideo. Possman Pat bideo.' After
six months of it, I'm beginning to develop a Postman
Pat phobia.

'It's too early to watch a video. Mummy's sleeping,
it's dark, look, even Teddy's sleeping, snore, snore,
snore.'

'No no no no no. No no no. Num nums.' (I must
remember to teach him the word for breakfast. He's far
to old to call it num nums still.)

'Play with your toys for an hour and Daddy will come
back. Daddy's sleeping too.'

'No. No. NO!'

And then, the look. The look, and the crumpling into
a wailing heap on the floor and facing Mecca. The look
that says 'If you walk out of that door and leave me
with my toys, I'm going to asphyxiate myself. I'm going
to scream and choke so loudly that the people below
will be sure that you're an abuser, and they'll call the
police, and Mummy will wake up and start crying and
blaming you, and I'll definitely be emotionally marked
for the rest of my life. Look, I'm already gasping for
breath, and streaming with snot, and IT'S YOUR
FAULT!'

Well, if you're that desperate for me to stay, it's very
flattering. Maybe I could just get a few minutes' kip

here on your miniature sofa, if I scrunch my legs up under me, and give myself a stiff neck on the teeny armrest.

'Choo-choo chain. Choo-choo chain', which he and I both know means 'OK, you can lie on my sofa, but you're going to have to read me a Thomas the Tank Engine book first. No. Two Thomas the Tank Engine books . . . twice.'

'Look, I'm really really really tired. I was out late last night. Stupid, I know, but I've got to do a whole day's work today as well.'

'Choo-choo chain, choo-choo chain, choo-choo chain.'

'Sssh, you'll wake Mummy up and then we'll both be sorry. Look here's your choo-choo train book, read it yourself. [I must remember to teach him to say train without the choo-choo prefix.] No, don't get our your jigsaws. Oh, what the hell. Muddle all the pieces up. I don't care.'

This mini-sofa isn't so bad. I think I could probably fall asleep quite easily here, if I just move the panda from under my shoulder . . . Ow! Who turned on the main light? 'Please turn off the light. No, It's not funny. My eyes hurt. What? You've got a sore ear? Show me. Well, you have got a cold at the moment. Let's wipe your nose. No, let me, OK, you do it. You do it properly. No, properly . . . Let Daddy do it then . . . Because I don't like having yellow snot all over my T-shirt. OK, I give up, let's have breakfast. It's five to six, but why not. As long as you're quiet, OK? Quiet. Yes. Ssshh.'

Great, he understands that. He makes big exaggerated shushing noises like in a Laurel and Hardy film, and having gathered together his engineer's hat, his Donald Duck, his teddy, his train books, and his fireman's helmet, we are ready to go to the kitchen. He tiptoes out into the corridor. As we go past the grown-up's bedroom door, he sits down and starts shouting. 'My car! My car!'

Oh my God, we forgot to bring his car! Shit! SHIT! 'And don't copy me when I say that.' Quick, back into the nursery . . . OK. Now you've got your car. Now drive it into the kitchen quickly. And don't bang it against all the doors. No, nor the walls.

'Mibena, Mibena.'

'OK, here's your Ribena.'

'Milk, Milk. No want Mibena.'

'Well, why didn't you say so? Here's your milk. Here's your num nums. [I mustn't keep calling it that.] What? You want toast instead? There's no need to shout about it. Here. Have mine. Why did you say Marmite if you wanted honey? No, you can't go and watch a video until you've eaten num nums, I mean breakfast, I mean toast. No, that's my new toast, and not on the floor, that's very naughty, [oooh, act shocked here] and where

do you think you're going? No, you can't put two videos
in the machine at once, take the other one out first, oh,
thank you for saying sorry, what a good boy, what a
clever boy for knowing where the eject button is on the
video, aaah, give us a big hug, oh, what a nice boy you
are after all, no, not the toast in the video, you won't be
able to watch Postman Pat, or Fireman Sam, and we'll
have to get the video repair man round for the fourth
time this week, and suffer those condescending looks he
gives us again. What? Bugger? What do you mean,
bugger? Who taught you that word? Bugger in the
kitchen? What do you mean? Bugger in the fridge? No,
don't open the fridge, no, put the milk down, what do
you mean, bugger? Point. Show me what you mean. Oh
. . . burger. Frozen burger. Frozen vegetable burger'.
Better check the ingredients for additives and Es.
Nothing too bad.

'You really want a burger? You haven't touched your
other food, and you've got to eat something. But it's
twenty-past six. Well, you haven't eaten anything else,
OK, I'll heat one up. Where have you gone? I don't like
that silence. No, not the answerphone, and never go
near a plug and never come in here, this is Daddy's
office – well, it's a shower room actually – and be quiet,
you'll wake Mummy up, what is it now? No, we're not
going shopping for bonbons. [Must remember to teach
him the word 'sweets', God knows why we did that one

in French.] And leave the letters alone, OK, put them in
your car, and come into the kitchen for your burger. Oh
bugger, the burger's burnt.'

It's only seven o'clock in the morning, and three
rooms are completely devastated. 'You want to play
jumping on the sofas? I though more a game of curling
up on the sofas. No? OK, you jump, I'll just sit here and
curl up, OK? And you jump on to me. No, don't pull my
face around like that, it hurts. [Must remember to cut
his fingernails soon.] Yes, I know it looks funny, yes,
Daddy has got a very silly rubbery face, yes it looks
funny, but it hurts a lot, especially at this time in the
morning. Yes, Daddy big, yes Daddy is big, big Daddy.
What's that? A laugh big Daddy? Oliver big Daddy?
Speak up . . . Elephant Daddy? A laffoo big Daddy. Ah
luff oo big Daddy. I luv you big Daddy. Who taught you
to say that?'

Oh God, this is really corny. He's actually saying
that. It's five past seven in the morning. And it's still
not light. I'm in a snot-covered stringy towelling
dressing gown, he stinks to high heaven, a full nappy,
and he's got flaky bits and gunge all over his cheeks.
Well, that's it. The high point in my life so far. That's
what the first thirty-five years have been leading to and
I've got about six and a half seconds to savour the
moment. I love you too, Stan. No, you can't have an
orange, and you shouldn't be in the fridge anyway, and

you know you're not allowed in that cupboard, don't you? Well, close the door and come out of there. Thank you. And what is this obsession with hats? OK, we'll go and get your other fireman hat, but BE QUIET IN THE CORRIDOR, no, not in the office, you've already got coins in your piggy bank . . . No, put the phone book back, you've got your own toy phone, why don't you play with that? Don't pull the plants apart . . .

And, no, you weren't a particularly hyper-active child . . .

'DADDY, WHAT COLOUR IS POSTMAN PAT'S WILLY?'

If men were capable of discussing sex as frankly as women are, there would be chapter headings in men's books like 'What to do when you get an unwanted erection'. Although we are accustomed to seeing women's bodies wrapped around the fish and chips or beavered across movie posters, there is still a taboo about the male member. Now that men are being encouraged to make more physical contact with their children, to bathe, change and cuddle more, there are decisions that have to be made over how to handle (if you will excuse the rather bad pun) this hitherto hidden problem.

You're in the bath with baby, who insisted on getting in there with you. There are bubbles, the scene looks idyllic, and could even be in one of those advertisements for designer soaps. Maybe mother is nearby, looking on, and then, for no reason at all, you get a stiffy, not a sexy stiffy, just a humdrum run-of-the-mill stiffy. Not because of the situation you're in, not really because of anything in particular, just one of those ordinary everyday erections that stick around pointlessly for a few minutes, and then go away again. This definitely does not fit into the cool new designer-image-dad commercial. What should you do? Conceal it from baby? Allow baby to see it and have a totally understanding talk about the birds and the bees? This is where all theories fall down. You cannot have a frank discussion with a toddler about your private parts and make a game out of them. That could be termed abuse.

In my parents' generation, penises and vaginas were definitely under-the-counter affairs and, so the argument goes, guilt, secrecy and taboos followed as one reached adolescence. In their day, for a dad to stand naked in front of his five-year-old daughter might have been considered abnormal. Then came the good old sixties, and secrecy and covering up became the dirty words.

A friend of mine has two daughters and a son. The little boy is fascinated by the way, he, unlike his sisters, can go to the toilet standing up. When he comes to play with Stanley, he watches in awe as I help Stanley take a wee-wee. His dad has decided to leave this particular activity to Mummy, until the boy is older. He has never seen his dad's willy. He is trying to work out who he is, and why he's different. None of us really knows what the right thing to do is.

This was a problem I wasn't expecting. One morning, I

what chocolate biscuit?

am lying in bed. It's summer, and I have no jimjams on. I have had rather a lot to drink the night before, and it's time to get up and have a pee. As you may or may not know, the penis, when in this situation, tends to become erect as a form of bladder control. Stanley is playing in the room. He is nearly two. Instinctively, I wrap the bedclothes around me, rather like women used to do in those coy TV plays that went out before the nine o'clock watershed, and thus gowned make my way to the toilet. It's easier to answer the question, 'Why are you dressing up in the bedclothes?' than it is, 'What's happened to your willy?' So, today I have found out where I draw the line. Up until now, Stanley has seen me naked, and I have answered all his questions about my anatomy. He has been delighted to find that he is 'the same' as his dad. 'I got willy, Daddy got willy.' And I think that until now openness has been the best policy.

In nonviolent, long-term abuse cases, evidently one of the problems social workers have is convincing children that a situation which has been 'normal' to them – in other words, everyday, – is actually an abnormal, abusive one. Once behaviour is learnt, it is sometimes impossibly difficult for people to redraw their map of the world without it. Several years ago, for me to have had any kind of physical contact with my child, other than that of the sporting or roughhouse kind, would have been considered abnormal.

By the time he was three, Buster Keaton was regularly appearing in his parents' vaudeville act, a knockabout comedy slapstick routine which consisted of him as a naughty child being hit and beaten with a broom, among other things, by his parents, without his batting an eyelid. Even as a child, his comedy came from his keeping a straight face. The authorities would often try to intervene because of the physical injuries he received, but the family were travelling players, and would move on to a new town before being apprehended. In his autobiography, *My Wonderful World of Slapstick*, Keaton describes his parents as his 'first bit of great luck': 'All the practical correction I ever received was with an audience looking on. I could not even wimper.' He interprets what we might call abuse as a wonderful training that helped him to develop his stony-faced comic persona. Should we attribute his later alcoholism and misery to this paradox, or just thank God that the social workers didn't get to him and attempt 'a cure', thus depriving us of some of the funniest films ever made?

PICKING GOOD GRANDPARENTS

By the time Stan is six months old, any criticisms of my own parents that I might still have, have completely evaporated. How did they cope with this? And they were younger than I am now when they had me and my brothers. Now I understand. At last. A quick action replay of my childhood and adolescence reveals that hitherto I have vastly misinterpreted them. Now I can see the other side of the coin, I have insight into the dilemmas they must have faced. They didn't know a thing about bringing up children either. No one does know until they've done it, it seems. I understand what my dad means when he says he is a better grandfather than he ever was a father.

The arrival of Stanley means that Anna and I see a lot more of our own parents. Not only because of their superb baby-minding and Sunday-lunch-making qualities, but also because we feel more connected to them now that we have a child of our own. When couples divorce, it is sad that so often their split deprives the child of one set of grandparents. Grandparents are very good things. Stanley's grandparents were the first people he could name after Mum and Dad, and his first example of homes outside his home. I never guessed how important they would be. I thought of having a child as something that would point only to the future; I did not see the bridge with the past which it illuminates.

Saying this makes me feel like the last five minutes of American comedy programmes, when the characters invariably stop the wise-cracking for a few moments in order to make inner realisations about themselves, and have heart-to-heart conversations with their loved ones that 'sort out all the problems' . . . 'I think we've learnt that sometimes you can be your own worst enemy.' Then they hug just long enough for the moral of the story to become grindingly apparent before the titles and the commercial break. But, seeing your child with its grandparents is blatantly sentimental. Being a grandparent seems to give people a certain dignity, which makes them twice as attractive as before. No doubt there are some awful ones somewhere, ones who interfere too much, or too little, but I haven't met any of them. So let's hear it for the grandparents! Yo! Whoop Whoop! . . . Music. Cut camera . . . Go to title sequence . . . And . . . commercial break.

When Stanley was about six months old, we went out together for an afternoon, leaving him at home with his grandma. Until then, it had been almost exclusively shiftwork. Either one of us would go away at a time, but rarely both. Up until then, he would not necessarily acknowledge us at departures or arrivals. He had not worked out that we could go and come back. No doubt he was pleased to see his mum, but he showed it in ways that were not easy for me to interpret. On this afternoon, when we returned, we walked into the room where he was playing with his gran, and for a few seconds he was unaware of our presence. Then he looked round and saw us standing in the doorway. His face lit up bigger than Christmas decorations, and, beaming, he dropped everything and crawled as fast as he could towards us, saying 'Mummy Daddy'. This thing masquerading as a person had recognised us and was pleased to see us. Suddenly I knew why we'd bothered to go through it all. There's no point in trying to explain the importance of that moment to me, and in any case, it would be about as uncliché-ridden as the translated lyrics of Turkey's entry for the Eurovision Song Contest.

A REST

It's a beautiful morning, judging by the sunlight straining through our curtains. And, yes, there are birds singing. How nice. No crying or calling from the next room to be heard yet. I must have woken up very early. Damn. I haven't had very much sleep all week; now I'll probably be dragging myself through the day. Stretch, roll over, look at watch. Eleven forty-five? Damn. Watch must have broken down again. Check with clock. Five-past twelve? Watch hasn't broken down, it's just slow. Five-past twelve? What? I leap out of bed. What am I meant to be doing today? Panic. Go into sitting room: no toys on floor. Kitchen: no mess. Go into Stanley's room. Have we all overslept? Stanley's bed is made. His curtains are open. Sunlight is blazing onto every neatly stacked toy basket and pop-up book. Teddies are sitting in orderly rows looking bored. There is no doubt about it. Stanley is not here.

Check the bedroom again to make sure Anna hasn't gone too. No, she's spark out under the duvet. Disorientated, I put on the kettle, and remember where I am. All is well. Stanley is staying with his granny. This is our first morning together at home without him for two years. We are due to go on holiday together for a week, and he is old enough to stay at his grandparents. We dropped him off a day early, to get a lie-in and pack in peace. Yesterday, after he had been delivered, and had cycled happily off into his gran's garden looking for snails, we found ourselves making plans for the evening in the usual way. 'I've got to pick up some things from work, but I can be back by four-thirty if you need to go out and drop off that table. So, if you get back by seven, that leaves us twenty-five minutes if we want to get to a film in time . . . hang on a minute . . . what am I saying? No Stanley. We can come and go as we please . . . Let's go to a film right now!'

Memories come flooding in of how easy arrangements used to be. Of the days when 'See you when I see you' was not a completely selfish thing to say. Anna and I have been running a campaign for three years. Someone has to be on the case at all times to pick him up, or to do the shopping. Will we have enough time to bath him and get to the party . . .? We tend to avoid the trendy 'Oh take your child with you anywhere' argument. People who invite you to impromptu parties and expect you to wake him up and drag him along with you because you can't find a baby-sitter that night, will not be the ones who have to cope with him the next day when he is tired and tearful from having his routine messed about. A child's timetable is very wearing on an adult if adhered to too strictly, but it seems to me that a child does like a timetable in which to explore. Stanley was lucky in that for the first two years of his life his mum created a solid and regular environment for him. My work hours are always changing – sometimes too late in the evening, sometimes ridiculously early in the morning – a difficult lifestyle to get even the sturdiest of biorhythms attuned to.

I pour myself a cup of coffee. I feel more seriously tired having had nine hours' sleep than if I'd got my usual six. Anna obviously feels the same, because the coffee I make her is allowed to go cold while she sleeps on. She can't catch up on two years' sleep in one night, but she's having a bloody good try. I walk around the flat looking at empty, tidy rooms. What did I use to do? Is this what it was like before? I am at a complete loss. Would I have just read the newspaper, put on some music, done some work, phoned some friends? I really can't remember. It's as if someone has pulled the plug on me, and everything's gone swirling down the drain. Without the constant noise and urgency, the chores to be done, I am an empty bath. Anna eventually gets up. We plod about in dressing gowns, and eat toast. All of the wonderful things one thinks one could do, if only the pressure were taken off, suddenly seem drab and lacklustre. We seem drab and lacklustre. What shall we do? Look at a few Postman Pat videos? No, that would be stupid.

After a boring hour, we catch each other's eyes and grin. We know without saying what we're going to do. We cuddle up on the sofa together . . .

. . . And telephone his granny to speak to him. 'Hello, what did you have for breakfast? Did you find any snails in the garden'? Are you having a nice time?' Honestly, What have we become?

I can't eat with you all watching

137

TEN

May 1992

Dear Stanley,

Maybe things will have changed by now, but when you were three it was unusual, if not unheard of, for little boys, when asked what they wanted to be when they grew up, to reply, 'I want to be a daddy'. In those dark days, apprentice men were still expected to dream only of driving trains, kicking balls or becoming movie directors. To be thought of as a caring man, it would have been enough to become a save-the-wildlife television presenter, or join the Liberal Democrats. The measure of the man still being defined by his work or his actions outside the family. There were very few generalised images of fatherhood on the market.

When you role-played Mummies and Daddies with little plastic people, I am pleased to say that the mums were not always nurses, nor the dads soldiers. From about nine months, however, you did appreciate that they were definitely different from one another.

The other day I found myself sitting next to an archetypal power-dressed eighties couple at a posh lunch launch to publicise some new piece of media thingummy or other. These people were in advertising. Or, more accurately, these people were advertising. They were up there with the high-flyers, their watches set to New York time, and their month's appointments logged on a Psion organiser. They could have read and digested a forty-page contract before their first breakfast appointment. You don't get where they'd got to by farting about having second thoughts, and introversion is a word they'd had deprogrammed from their hard disks when they left school. They made a lot of money. Even, it seemed, in the recession. A 50 per cent cut in their salaries would probably have brought them down to the level of a Viking warlord charging Danegeld.

Running out of common interests about which to make polite conversation took about three and a half minutes, so I asked if they had any children. They had a son of five, whom they did not see for as much as three weeks at a time. Well, they saw him, they explained, but by the time they got in, the child was asleep, and likewise when they left in the morning. 'How is it for you?' I asked. 'How does it make you feel?'

'Oh, no problem,' they replied with bravado. 'Our son knows who we are and he loves his nanny.'

The nanny, it turned out, was nineteen, and had a boyfriend. Immediately, I worried about whether the nanny would get pregnant, or want to travel, or follow her boyfriend to a new town. But then I'm like that. I am a fusser and a worrier. They don't call me Niggle Complainer for nothing, and I found myself thinking, 'This is terrible. The poor child, the poor deluded parents. Do they really have to work so hard? What kind of example are they setting? Don't they know what they're missing out on? Don't they know Mrs Thatcher resigned? It's the nineties now for goodness sake . . .' But to each his or her own. *I probably wouldn't get very far in the world of international advertising. Maybe I should have been sat next to someone else.*

Now that it looks like you're going to be a father yourself, I hope I haven't made it all sound too ghastly by exaggerating the bad things to get cheap laughs. The trouble is, most of the really good things about it are as boring to everyone but myself and your mum as that endless video we took of you in your Baby-bouncer when you were eight months old. Personally, I could watch that for hours, but I'm not sure that it would make exciting television for anyone else.

However, what that couple were missing out on was things like: 'Daddy, a monster's eaten my holiday', and 'Whobody else is coming to my party?', and 'How will we see with the dark on?', and 'Flowers don't have bosoms, do they' and (a description of water) 'Zero colour', and 'I'll be nearly four for a very long time', and (every time we pass a cinema) 'Am I eighteen yet?'

The good things happened every day. Every time you discovered something new or made us laugh. Like standing in your fireman's hat with a Red Indian feather in your hand, trying to tickle the monsters out from under your bed; like your insistence that to be a cowboy you had to have a cowboy hat and a cowboy ticket (ticket? you used an out-of-date Musicians' Union card); like the first time you encountered a Sindy doll, ripped off its blouse, and used it upside down as a toy Hoover; like your first Christmas carol, 'Away in a Manger', in which the little Lord Jesus 'lay down in his boot'; like your first practical joke, when you held your mug behind your back and asked us, 'Where's my mug?' (we fell for it); like the time you farted in the crowded lift and said, 'I just did a little bottom burp. I'm saving the big one for when I get home, like Daddy.'

I have found being your dad the most paradoxical time of my life to date, bringing out both the best and worst in me. Sometimes it made what I thought was my best seem totally inadequate, and my worst, quite sensible. Life, the Universe, those little bits of blue fluff you get in your navel, all began at last to make sense at the same time as becoming twice as confusing and annoying. Now that you are about to set off on this road yourself, one final piece of advice: never agree to write a book about it.

Sorry if I wasted your time.

Dad